YOUR
BIBLE

YOUR BIBLE

An Easy-to-Understand Guide to God's Word

BARBOUR
PUBLISHING

© 2012 by Barbour Publishing, Inc.

Print ISBN 978-1-61626-950-0

ebook Editions:
Adobe Digital Edition (.epub) 978-1-62029-406-2
Kindle and MobiPocket Edition (.prc) 978-1-62029-405-5

Published by Barbour Publishing, Inc., P.O. Box 719, Uhrichsville, Ohio 44683, www.barbourbooks.com

Our mission is to publish and distribute inspirational products offering exceptional value and biblical encouragement to the masses.

 Member of the
Evangelical Christian
Publishers Association

Printed in the United States of America.

CONTENTS

INTRODUCTION

This book provides clear, easy-to-understand information about the Bible—highlights of what's in it, where the Bible comes from, how to study scripture, and how to memorize verses. But please don't stop with this book!

Don't just read *about* the Bible, read the Bible itself. Don't just know *facts* about scripture—know scripture. Take what you learn in this book and put it into practice in regular Bible reading, study, memorization, and meditation.

Let's consider these practices one by one:

1. *Read the Bible*—That sounds pretty basic, but in truth, few Christians have taken the time to simply read the Bible cover to cover. One of the benefits of reading the Bible this way is that you get a great overview of the complete story it has to tell. Try reading through the Bible in conjunction with the first section of this book, ***Know Your Bible.***

2. *Study the Bible*—There are several methods for studying the Bible, and all of them can be of great benefit in your walk of faith. The second section of this book, ***How to Study the Bible,*** explains the various methods for digging deeper into God's Word—deductive study, inductive study, word study, and more. It also describes the essential tools for the process— study Bibles, concordances, Bible dictionaries, and a reliable Bible commentary.

3. *Memorize the Bible*—The apostle Peter instructed believers to "always be ready to give a defense to everyone who asks you a reason for the hope that is in you" (1 Peter 3:15 NKJV). The best way to follow that important bit of instruction is to commit portions of the Bible to memory. The third section of this book, **Bible Memory Plan**, will give you 52 key verses—one for each week of the year—along with tips and techniques to help you in your effort.

4. *Meditate on the Bible*—The Bible clearly teaches that there is great blessing and power in meditating on God's Word: "Blessed is the man who walks not in the counsel of the ungodly, nor stands in the path of sinners, nor sits in the seat of the scornful; but his delight is in the law of the LORD, and in His law he meditates day and night" (Psalm 1:1–2 NKJV). In this context, *meditation* means to think deeply about something, to ponder it and consider what it means to you, and—most importantly—to dwell on what the book's Author is saying to you personally. The fourth section of this book, **How Did We Get the Bible?**, will give you great confidence that the scriptures you're contemplating originated with God Himself, who guarded them through the centuries for your benefit today.

The Bible is no ordinary book; it is the result of the mouth of God speaking and the hand of God orchestrating events as only He can—so we would have His written Word to guide our thoughts, our words, and our actions, so that all we think, say, or do pleases Him.

Knowing what God has done to give us the Bible *and* what applying the principles, commands, and promises of the Bible can do for our walk of faith should motivate every believer to make the Bible a central part of his or her life of faith in Jesus Christ.

Know Your Bible

All 66 Books Explained and Applied

Paul Kent

Contents

INTRODUCTION

Through sixty-six separate books, 1,189 chapters, and hundreds of thousands of words, the Bible shares one extraordinary message: God loves you.

From the first chapter of Genesis, where God creates human beings, through the last chapter of Revelation, where God welcomes anyone to "take the water of life freely" (22:17), the Bible proves God is intimately involved in, familiar with, and concerned about the lives of people. His amazing love is shown in the death of His Son, Jesus Christ, on the cross. That sacrifice for sin allows anyone to be right with God through simple faith in Jesus' work.

These truths are found in the pages of scripture. But sometimes they can be obscured by the vast amount of information the Bible contains. That's why *Know Your Bible* was written.

In this little book, you'll find brief surveys of all sixty-six Bible books. Each summarizes what that book is about—always within the context of God's love and concern for people. Every entry follows this outline:

- AUTHOR: who wrote the book, according to the Bible itself or ancient tradition.

- DATE: when the book was written or the time the book covers.

- IN TEN WORDS OR LESS: a "nutshell" glance at the book's key theme.

- DETAILS, PLEASE: a synopsis of the key people, events, and messages covered in the book.

- QUOTABLE: one, two, or several key verses from the book.

- UNIQUE AND UNUSUAL: facts—some serious, some less so—that make the book stand out.

- SO WHAT? an inspirational or devotional thought for each book.

Your Bible is certainly worth knowing. Use this book to begin a journey of discovery that could truly change your life!

GENESIS

AUTHOR
Not stated but traditionally attributed to Moses.

DATE
Moses lived around the 1400s BC, but the events of Genesis date to the very beginning of time.

IN TEN WORDS OR LESS
God creates the world and chooses a special people.

DETAILS, PLEASE
The Bible's first book never explains God; it simply assumes His existence: "In the beginning, God. . ." (1:1). Chapters 1 and 2 describe how God created the universe and everything in it simply by speaking: "God said. . .and it was so" (1:6–7, 9, 11, 14–15). Humans, however, received special handling, as "God formed man of the dust of the ground, and breathed into his nostrils the breath of life" (2:7), and woman was crafted from a rib of man. Those first two people, Adam and Eve, live in perfection but ruined paradise by disobeying God at the urging of a "subtil" (crafty, 3:1) serpent. Sin throws humans into a moral freefall as the world's first child—Cain—murders his brother Abel. People become so bad that God decides to flood the entire planet, saving only the righteous Noah, his family, and an ark (boat) full of animals. After the earth repopulates, God chooses a man named Abram as patriarch of a specially blessed people, later called "Israel" after an alternative name of Abram's grandson Jacob. Genesis ends with Jacob's son Joseph, by a miraculous chain of events, ruling in Egypt—setting up the events of the following book of Exodus.

QUOTABLE
God said, Let there be light: and there was light. (1:3)

The LORD said unto Cain, Where is Abel thy brother? And he said, I know not: Am I my brother's keeper? (4:9)

Noah found grace in the eyes of the LORD. (6:8)

He [Abram] believed in the LORD; and he counted it to him for righteousness. (15:6)

UNIQUE AND UNUSUAL
Genesis quickly introduces the concept of one God in multiple persons, a concept later called the Trinity: "God said, Let us make man in our image, after our likeness" (1:26, emphasis added). Also early on, God gives a hint of Jesus' future suffering and victory when He curses the serpent for deceiving

Eve: "I will put enmity between thee and the woman, and between thy seed and her seed; it shall bruise thy head, and thou shalt bruise his heel" (3:15).

So What?
Genesis answers the great question "Where did I come from?" Knowing the answer can give us meaning in a world that's otherwise hard to figure out.

Exodus

Author
Not stated but traditionally attributed to Moses. In Exodus 34:27 God tells Moses, "Write thou these words," and Jesus, in Mark 12:26, quotes from Exodus as "the book of Moses."

Date
Approximately the mid-1400s BC.

In Ten Words or Less
God delivers His people, the Israelites, from slavery in Egypt.

Details, Please
The Israelites prosper in Egypt, having settled there at the invitation of Abraham's great-grandson Joseph, who entered the country as a slave and rose to second in command. When Joseph dies, a new pharaoh sees the burgeoning family as a threat—and makes the people his slaves. God hears the Israelites' groaning, remembering "his covenant with Abraham, with Isaac, and with Jacob" (2:24) and raising up Moses as their deliverer. God speaks through a burning bush, and Moses reluctantly agrees to demand the Israelites' release from Pharaoh. To break Pharaoh's will, God sends ten plagues on Egypt, ending with the death of every firstborn child—except those of the Israelites. They put sacrificial blood on their doorposts, causing the Lord to "pass over" (12:13) their homes. Pharaoh finally allows the Israelites to leave the country (the "Exodus"), and God parts the Red Sea for the people, who are being pursued by Egyptian soldiers. At Mount Sinai, God delivers the Ten Commandments, rules for worship, and laws to change the family into a nation. When Moses delays on the mountain, the people begin worshipping a golden calf, bringing a plague upon themselves. Moses returns to restore order, and Exodus ends with the people continuing their journey to the "promised land" of Canaan, following God's "pillar of cloud" by day and "pillar of fire" by night.

Quotable
God said unto Moses, I AM THAT I AM: and he said, Thus shalt thou say unto the children of Israel, I AM hath sent me unto you. (3:14)

Thus saith the Lord, Let my people go. (8:1)

When I see the blood, I will pass over you. (12:13)

Thou shalt have no other gods before me. (20:3)

UNIQUE AND UNUSUAL
God told the Israelites to celebrate the "Passover" with a special meal of bread made without yeast (12:14–15). Three thousand years later, Jewish people still commemorate the event.

SO WHAT?
The story of redemption is on clear display in Exodus as God rescues His people from their slavery in Egypt. In the same way, Jesus breaks our bonds of sin (Hebrews 2:14–15).

LEVITICUS

AUTHOR
Not stated but traditionally attributed to Moses.

DATE
Approximately the mid-1400s BC.

IN TEN WORDS OR LESS
A holy God explains how to worship Him.

DETAILS, PLEASE
Leviticus, meaning "about the Levites," describes how that family line should lead the Israelites in worship. The book provides ceremonial laws as opposed to the moral laws of Exodus, describing offerings to God, dietary restrictions, and purification rites. Special holy days—including the Sabbath, Passover, and Day of Atonement (Yom Kippur)—are commanded. The family of Aaron, Moses' brother, is ordained as Israel's formal priesthood. Leviticus lists several blessings for obedience and many more punishments for disobedience.

QUOTABLE
Ye shall be holy; for I [God] am holy. (11:44)

The life of the flesh is in the blood. . .it is the blood that maketh an atonement for the soul. (17:11)

UNIQUE AND UNUSUAL
Leviticus's blood sacrifices are contrasted with Jesus' death on the cross by the writer of Hebrews: "Who needeth not daily, as those high priests, to offer up sacrifice. . .for this he did once, when he offered up himself" (7:27).

SO WHAT?
Though we don't live under the rules of Leviticus, we still serve a holy God—and should treat Him as such.

NUMBERS

AUTHOR
Not stated but traditionally attributed to Moses.

DATE
Approximately 1400 BC.

IN TEN WORDS OR LESS
Faithless Israelites wander forty years in the wilderness of Sinai.

DETAILS, PLEASE
Numbers begins with a census—hence the book's name. Fourteen months after the Israelites escape Egypt, they number 603,550 men, not including the Levites. This mass of people, the newly formed nation of Israel, begins a march of approximately two hundred miles to the "promised land" of Canaan—a journey that will take decades to complete. The delay is God's punishment of the people, who complain about food and water, rebel against Moses, and hesitate to enter Canaan because of powerful people already living there. God decrees that this entire generation will die in the wilderness, leaving the Promised Land to a new generation of more obedient Israelites.

QUOTABLE
The LORD is longsuffering, and of great mercy, forgiving iniquity and transgression. (14:18)

UNIQUE AND UNUSUAL
Even Moses misses out on the Promised Land, punishment for disobeying God by striking, rather than speaking to, a rock from which water would miraculously appear (20:1–13).

SO WHAT?
God hates sin and punishes it. We can be thankful that Jesus took that punishment for us.

DEUTERONOMY

AUTHOR
Traditionally attributed to Moses, an idea supported by Deuteronomy 31:9: "Moses wrote this law, and delivered it unto the priests. . .and unto all the elders of Israel." Chapter 34, recording Moses' death, was probably written by his successor, Joshua.

DATE
Approximately 1400 BC.

IN TEN WORDS OR LESS
Moses reminds the Israelites of their history and God's laws.

DETAILS, PLEASE
With a name meaning "second law," Deuteronomy records Moses' final words as the Israelites prepare to enter the Promised Land. Forty years have passed since God handed down His laws on Mount Sinai, and the entire generation that experienced that momentous event has died. So Moses reminds the new generation both of God's commands and of their national history as they ready their entry into Canaan. The invasion will occur under Joshua, as Moses will only *see* the Promised Land from Mount Nebo. "So Moses the servant of the LORD died there. . . . And he [God] buried him in a valley in the land of Moab. . .but no man knoweth of his sepulchre unto this day" (34:5–6). Moses was 120 years old.

QUOTABLE
Hear, O Israel: The LORD our God is one LORD. (6:4)

Thou shalt love the LORD thy God with all thine heart, and with all thy soul, and with all thy might. (6:5)

The LORD thy God is a jealous God among you. (6:15)

UNIQUE AND UNUSUAL
The New Testament quotes from Deuteronomy dozens of times, including three from the story of Jesus' temptation in the wilderness in Matthew 4:1–11. The Lord defeated Satan by restating Deuteronomy 8:3 ("Man shall not live by bread alone, but by every word that proceedeth out of the mouth of God"); 6:16 ("Thou shalt not tempt the Lord thy God"); and 6:13 ("Thou shalt worship the Lord thy God, and him only shalt thou serve").

The Ten Commandments, most commonly found in Exodus 20, are restated in full in Deuteronomy 5.

SO WHAT?
Deuteronomy makes clear that God's rules and expectations aren't meant to limit and frustrate us but instead to benefit us: "Hear therefore, O Israel, and observe to do it; that it may be well with thee, and that ye may increase mightily, as the LORD God of thy fathers hath promised thee, in the land that floweth with milk and honey" (6:3).

JOSHUA

AUTHOR
Traditionally attributed to Joshua himself, except for the final five verses (24:29–33), which describe Joshua's death and legacy.

DATE
Approximately 1375 BC.

IN TEN WORDS OR LESS
The Israelites capture and settle the promised land of Canaan.

DETAILS, PLEASE
With Moses and an entire generation of disobedient Israelites dead, God tells Joshua to lead the people into Canaan, their promised land. In Jericho, the first major obstacle, the prostitute Rahab helps Israelite spies and earns protection from the destruction of the city: God knocks its walls flat as Joshua's army marches outside, blowing trumpets and shouting. Joshua leads a successful military campaign to clear idol-worshipping people—Hittites, Amorites, Canaanites, Perizzites, Hivites, and Jebusites—from the land. At one point, God answers Joshua's prayer to make the sun stand still, allowing more time to complete a battle (10:1–15). Major cities subdued, Joshua divides the land among the twelve tribes of Israel, reminding the people to stay true to the God who led them home: "Now therefore put away. . .the strange gods which are among you, and incline your heart unto the LORD God of Israel" (24:23).

QUOTABLE
Be strong and of a good courage; be not afraid, neither be thou dismayed: for the LORD thy God is with thee whithersoever thou goest. (1:9)

One man of you shall chase a thousand: for the LORD your God, he it is that fighteth for you, as he hath promised you. (23:10)

Choose you this day whom ye will serve. . .as for me and my house, we will serve the LORD. (24:15)

UNIQUE AND UNUSUAL
Joshua is one of few major Bible characters who seemed to do everything right—he was a strong leader, completely committed to God, who never fell into recorded sin or disobedience. Only one mistake mars his record: Joshua's experience with the Gibeonites, one of the local groups he should have destroyed. Fearing for their lives, they appeared before Joshua dressed in old clothes, carrying dry, moldy bread, claiming they had come from a faraway land. Joshua and the Israelite leaders "asked not counsel at the mouth of the LORD" (9:14) and agreed to a peace treaty. When Joshua learned the truth, he honored his agreement with the Gibeonites—but made them slaves.

SO WHAT?
Joshua shows over and over how God blesses His people. The Promised Land was His gift to them, as were the military victories that He engineered.

JUDGES

AUTHOR
Unknown; some suggest the prophet Samuel.

DATE
Written approximately 1050 BC, covering events that occurred as far back as 1375 BC.

IN TEN WORDS OR LESS
Israel goes through cycles of sin, suffering, and salvation.

DETAILS, PLEASE
After Joshua's death, the Israelites lose momentum in driving pagan people out of the Promised Land. "The children of Benjamin did not drive out the Jebusites that inhabited Jerusalem" (1:21) is a statement characteristic of many tribes, which allow idol worshippers to stay in their midst—with tragic results. "Ye have not obeyed my voice" God says to His people. "They shall be as thorns in your sides, and their gods shall be a snare unto you" (2:2–3). That's exactly what happens, as the Israelites begin a cycle of worshipping idols, suffering punishment by attackers, crying to God for help, and receiving God's aid in the form of a human judge (or "deliverer") who restores order. Lesser-known judges include Othniel, Ehud, Tola, Jair, and Jephthah, while more familiar figures are Deborah, the only female judge, who led a military victory against the Canaanites; Gideon, who tested God's will with a fleece and defeated the armies of Midian; and the amazingly strong Samson, who defeated the Philistines. Samson's great weakness—his love for unsavory women such as Delilah—led to his downfall and death in a Philistine temple.

QUOTABLE
They forsook the LORD God of their fathers, which brought them out of the land of Egypt, and followed other gods, of the gods of the people that were round about them. (2:12)

The LORD raised up judges, which delivered them out of the hand of those that spoiled them. (2:16)

The LORD said unto Gideon, The people that are with thee are too many for me to give the Midianites into their hands, lest Israel vaunt themselves against me, saying, Mine own hand hath saved me. (7:2)

UNIQUE AND UNUSUAL
Several judges had unusual families by today's standards: Jair had thirty sons (10:4), Abdon had forty sons (12:14), and Ibzan had thirty sons and thirty daughters (12:9). Jephthah had only one child, a daughter, whom he foolishly vowed to sacrifice to God in exchange for a military victory (11:30–40).

So What?

The ancient Israelites got into trouble when they "did that which was right in [their] own eyes" (17:6; 21:25) rather than what God wanted them to do. Don't make the same mistake yourself!

Ruth

Author

Not stated; some suggest Samuel.

Date

Ruth, the great-grandmother of King David (who reigned approximately 1010–970 BC), probably lived around 1100 BC.

In Ten Words or Less

Loyal daughter-in-law pictures God's faithfulness, love, and care.

Details, Please

Ruth, a Gentile woman, marries into a Jewish family. When all of the men of the family die, Ruth shows loyalty to her mother-in-law, Naomi, staying with her and scavenging food to keep them alive. As Ruth gleans barley in a field of the wealthy Boaz, he takes an interest in her and orders his workers to watch over her. Naomi recognizes Boaz as her late husband's relative and encourages Ruth to pursue him as a "kinsman redeemer," one who weds a relative's widow to continue a family line. Boaz marries Ruth, starting a prominent family.

Quotable

Whither thou goest, I will go; and where thou lodgest, I will lodge: thy people shall be my people, and thy God my God. (1:16)

Unique and Unusual

Ruth, from the pagan land of Moab, married a Jewish man and became the great-grandmother of Israel's greatest king, David—and an ancestor of Jesus Christ.

So What?

We can trust God to provide what we need, when we need it—and to work out our lives in ways that are better than we ever imagined.

1 Samuel

Author

Not stated. Samuel himself was likely involved, though some of the history of 1 Samuel occurs after the prophet's death.

Date

Approximately 1100–1000 BC.

IN TEN WORDS OR LESS
Israel's twelve tribes unite under a king.

DETAILS, PLEASE
An infertile woman, Hannah, begs God for a son, promising to return him to the Lord's service. Samuel is born and soon sent to the temple to serve under the aging priest, Eli. Upon Eli's death, Samuel serves as judge, or deliverer, of Israel, subduing the nation's fearsome enemy, the Philistines. As Samuel ages, Israel's tribal leaders reject his sinful sons and ask for a king. Samuel warns that a king will tax the people and force them into service, but they insist and God tells Samuel to anoint the notably tall and handsome Saul as Israel's first ruler. King Saul starts well but begins making poor choices—and when he offers a sacrifice to God, a job reserved for priests, Samuel tells Saul that he will be replaced. Saul's successor will be a shepherd named David, who with God's help kills a giant Philistine warrior named Goliath and becomes Israel's hero. The jealous king seeks to kill David, who runs for his life. David rejects opportunities to kill Saul himself, saying, "I would not stretch forth mine hand against the LORD's anointed" (26:23). At the end of 1 Samuel, Saul dies battling the Philistines, making way for David to become king.

QUOTABLE
The LORD said unto Samuel. . .they have not rejected thee, but they have rejected me, that I should not reign over them. (8:7)

Behold, to obey is better than sacrifice, and to hearken than the fat of rams. (15:22)

Then said David to the Philistine [Goliath], Thou comest to me with a sword, and with a spear, and with a shield: but I come to thee in the name of the LORD of hosts, the God of the armies of Israel, whom thou hast defied. (17:45)

UNIQUE AND UNUSUAL
The future King Saul is a donkey herder (9:5) who tries to hide from his own coronation (10:21–22). As king, Saul breaks his own law by asking a medium to call up the spirit of the dead Samuel (chapter 28).

SO WHAT?
Selfish choices—such as the Israelites' request for a king and Saul's decision to offer a sacrifice he had no business making—can have heavy, even tragic, consequences.

2 SAMUEL

AUTHOR
Unknown but not Samuel—since the events of the book take place after his death. Some suggest Abiathar the priest (15:35).

Date
Approximately 1010–970 BC, the reign of King David.

In Ten Words or Less
David becomes Israel's greatest king—but with major flaws.

Details, Please
When King Saul dies, David is made king by the southern Jewish tribe of Judah. Seven years later, after the death of Saul's son Ish-bosheth, king of the northern tribes, David becomes ruler of all Israel. Capturing Jerusalem from the Jebusites, David creates a new capital for his unified nation, and God promises David, "Your throne will be established forever" (7:16 NIV). Military victories make Israel strong, but when David stays home from battle one spring, he commits adultery with a beautiful neighbor, Bathsheba. Then he has her husband—one of his soldiers—murdered. The prophet Nathan confronts David with a story of a rich man who steals a poor man's sheep. David is furious until Nathan announces, "Thou art the man" (12:7). Chastened, David repents and God forgives his sins—but their consequences will affect David powerfully. The baby conceived in the tryst dies, and David's family begins to splinter apart. One of David's sons, Amnon, rapes his half sister, and a second son, Absalom—full brother to the violated girl—kills Amnon in revenge. Absalom then conspires to steal the kingdom from David, causing his father to flee for his life. When Absalom dies in battle with David's men, David grieves so deeply that he offends his soldiers. Ultimately, David returns to Jerusalem to reassert his kingship. He also raises another son born to Bathsheba—Solomon.

Quotable
How are the mighty fallen in the midst of the battle! (1:25)

Who am I, O Lord GOD? and what is my house, that thou hast brought me hitherto? (7:18)

O my son Absalom, my son, my son Absalom! would God I had died for thee, O Absalom, my son, my son! (18:33)

Unique and Unusual
David's nephew killed a Philistine "of great stature, that had on every hand six fingers, and on every foot six toes" (21:20). David's top soldier, Adino, once killed 800 men single-handedly (23:8).

So What?
King David's story highlights the vital importance of the choices we make. Who would have guessed that such a great man could fall into such terrible sin?

1 Kings

Author
Not stated and unknown; one early tradition claimed Jeremiah wrote 1 and 2 Kings.

Date
Covering events from about 970 to 850 BC, 1 Kings was probably written sometime after the Babylonian destruction of Jerusalem in 586 BC.

In Ten Words or Less
Israel divides into rival northern and southern nations.

Details, Please
King David, in declining health, names Solomon, his son with Bathsheba, successor. After David's death, God speaks to Solomon in a dream, offering him anything he'd like—and Solomon chooses wisdom. God gives Solomon great wisdom, along with much power and wealth. The new king soon builds God a permanent temple in Jerusalem, and the Lord visits Solomon again to promise blessings for obedience and trouble for disobedience. Sadly, Solomon's wisdom fails him, as he marries seven hundred women, many of them foreigners who turn his heart to idols. When Solomon dies, his son Rehoboam foolishly antagonizes the people of Israel, and ten northern tribes form their own nation under Jeroboam, a former official of Solomon's. Two southern tribes continue under Solomon's line in a nation called Judah. Jeroboam begins badly, initiating idol worship in the north; many wicked rulers follow. Judah will also have many poor leaders, though occasional kings, such as Asa and Jehoshaphat, follow the Lord. 1 Kings introduces the prophet Elijah, who confronts the evil King Ahab and Queen Jezebel of Israel regarding their worship of the false god Baal. In God's power, Elijah defeats 450 false prophets in a dramatic contest on Mount Carmel.

Quotable
David drew nigh that he should die; and he charged Solomon his son, saying, I go the way of all the earth: be thou strong therefore, and shew thyself a man. (2:1–2)

Give therefore thy servant an understanding heart to judge thy people, that I may discern between good and bad: for who is able to judge this thy so great a people? (3:9)

Hear me, O Lord, hear me, that this people may know that thou art the Lord God, and that thou hast turned their heart back again. (18:37)

Unique and Unusual
Scholars say 1 and 2 Kings were originally a single volume and were split in half to allow for copying onto normal-sized scrolls.

So What?

Solomon's example provides a strong warning: Even the most blessed person can drift from God and make big mistakes.

2 Kings

Author

Not stated and unknown; one early tradition claimed Jeremiah wrote 1 and 2 Kings.

Date

Covering about three hundred years from the 800s BC on, 2 Kings was probably written sometime after the Babylonian destruction of Jerusalem in 586 BC.

In Ten Words or Less

Both Jewish nations are destroyed for their disobedience to God.

Details, Please

The story of 1 Kings continues, with more bad rulers, a handful of good ones, some familiar prophets, and the ultimate loss of the two Jewish nations. Early in 2 Kings, Elijah becomes the second man (after Enoch in Genesis 5:24) to go straight to heaven without dying. His successor, Elisha, performs many miracles and shares God's word with the "average people" of Israel. The northern kingdom's rulers are entirely wicked, and Israel, under its last king, Hoshea, is "carried. . .away into Assyria" (17:6) in 722 BC. Judah, with occasional good kings such as Hezekiah and Josiah, lasts a few years longer—but in 586 BC the southern kingdom's capital of Jerusalem "was broken up" (25:4) by Babylonian armies under King Nebuchadnezzar. Besides taking everything valuable from the temple and the Jewish king's palace, the Babylonians also "carried away all Jerusalem, and all the princes, and all the mighty men of valour, even ten thousand captives, and all the craftsmen and smiths" (24:14). Ending on a slight up note, 2 Kings describes a new king of Babylon, Evil-merodach, showing kindness to Jehoiachin, the last real king of Judah, by giving him a place of honor in the Babylonian court.

Quotable

Behold, there appeared a chariot of fire, and horses of fire, and parted them both asunder; and Elijah went up by a whirlwind into heaven. (2:11)

The LORD rejected all the seed of Israel, and afflicted them, and delivered them into the hand of spoilers, until he had cast them out of his sight. (17:20)

So Judah was carried away out of their land. (25:21)

Unique and Unusual

Isaiah, who wrote a long prophecy that appears later in the Old Testament, is prominent in 2 Kings 19. One of Judah's best kings, Josiah, was only eight years old when he took the throne (22:1).

So What?
Both Israel and Judah found that there were terrible consequences to sin. Even bad examples can be helpful if we decide not to do the things that bring us trouble.

1 Chronicles

Author
Not stated but traditionally attributed to Ezra the priest.

Date
Covers the history of Israel from about 1010 BC (the death of King Saul) to about 970 BC (the death of King David).

In Ten Words or Less
King David's reign is detailed and analyzed.

Details, Please
1 Chronicles provides a history of Israel, going as far back as Adam. By the eleventh chapter, the story turns to Israel's greatest king, David, with special emphasis on his leadership of national worship. Another important focus is on God's promise that David would have an eternal kingly line through his descendant Jesus Christ.

Quotable
I will settle him in mine house and in my kingdom for ever: and his throne shall be established for evermore. (17:14)

Unique and Unusual
1 Chronicles covers much of the same information as 2 Samuel, but without some of the seedier aspects of David's life—such as his adultery with Bathsheba and the engineered killing of her husband, Uriah.

So What?
The positive spin of 1 Chronicles was designed to remind the Jews that despite their punishment for sin, they were still God's special people. When God makes a promise, He keeps it.

2 Chronicles

Author
Not stated but traditionally attributed to Ezra the priest.

DATE

Covers Israelite history from about 970 BC (the accession of King Solomon) to the 500s BC (when exiled Jews returned to Jerusalem).

IN TEN WORDS OR LESS

The history of Israel from Solomon to division to destruction.

DETAILS, PLEASE

David's son Solomon is made king, builds the temple, and becomes one of the most prominent rulers ever. But when he dies, the Jewish nation divides. In the remainder of 2 Chronicles, the various kings of the relatively godlier southern nation of Judah are profiled right down to the destruction of Jerusalem by the Babylonians. The book ends with the Persian king Cyrus allowing Jews to rebuild the devastated temple.

QUOTABLE

O LORD God of Israel, there is no God like thee in the heaven, nor in the earth; which keepest covenant, and shewest mercy unto thy servants, that walk before thee with all their hearts. (6:14)

UNIQUE AND UNUSUAL

Continuing the positive spin of 1 Chronicles (the two books were originally one), 2 Chronicles ends with two verses that exactly repeat the first three verses of Ezra.

SO WHAT?

God's punishment isn't intended to hurt people but to bring them back to Him.

EZRA

AUTHOR

Not stated but traditionally attributed to Ezra the priest (7:11).

DATE

Approximately 530 BC to the mid-400s BC.

IN TEN WORDS OR LESS

Spiritual renewal begins after the Jews return from exile.

DETAILS, PLEASE

About a half century after Babylonians sacked Jerusalem and carried Jews into captivity, Persia is the new world power. King Cyrus allows a group of exiles to return to Judah to rebuild the temple. Some 42,000 people return and resettle the land. About seventy years later, Ezra is part of a smaller group that also returns. He teaches the law to the people, who have fallen away from God to the point of intermarrying with nearby pagan nations, something that was strictly forbidden by Moses (Deuteronomy 7:1–3).

QUOTABLE
Ezra had prepared his heart to seek the law of the LORD, and to do it, and to teach in Israel statutes and judgments. (7:10)

UNIQUE AND UNUSUAL
Though God has said, "I hate divorce" (Malachi 2:16 NIV), Ezra urged Jewish men to separate from their foreign wives.

SO WHAT?
In Ezra, God shows His willingness to offer a second chance—allowing a nation that had been punished for disobedience to have a fresh start. Guess what? He's still in the second-chance business.

NEHEMIAH

AUTHOR
"The words of Nehemiah" (1:1), though Jewish tradition says those words were put on paper by Ezra.

DATE
Approximately 445 BC.

IN TEN WORDS OR LESS
Returning Jewish exiles rebuild the broken walls of Jerusalem.

DETAILS, PLEASE
Nehemiah serves as "the king's cupbearer" (1:11) in Shushan, Persia. As a Jew, he's disturbed to learn that even though exiles have been back in Judah for nearly a hundred years, they have not rebuilt the city's walls, devastated by the Babylonians in 586 BC. Nehemiah asks and receives the king's permission to return to Jerusalem, where he leads a team of builders—against much pagan opposition—in reconstructing the walls in only fifty-two days. The quick work on the project shocks the Jews' enemies, who "perceived that this work was wrought of our God" (6:16).

QUOTABLE
Think upon me, my God, for good, according to all that I have done for this people. (5:19)

UNIQUE AND UNUSUAL
Indignant over some fellow Jews' intermarriage with pagans, Nehemiah "cursed them, and smote certain of them, and plucked off their hair" (13:25).

SO WHAT?
Nehemiah's success in rebuilding Jerusalem's walls provides many leadership principles for today—especially his consistent focus on prayer.

ESTHER

AUTHOR
Not stated but perhaps Ezra or Nehemiah.

DATE
Approximately 486–465 BC, during the reign of King Ahasuerus of Persia. Esther became queen around 479 BC.

IN TEN WORDS OR LESS
Beautiful Jewish girl becomes queen, saves fellow Jews from slaughter.

DETAILS, PLEASE
In a nationwide beauty contest, young Esther becomes queen of Persia without revealing her Jewish heritage. When a royal official plots to kill every Jew in the country, Esther risks her own life to request the king's protection. The king, pleased with Esther, is shocked by his official's plan and has the man hanged—while decreeing that the Jews should defend themselves against the planned slaughter. Esther's people prevail and commemorate the event with a holiday called Purim.

QUOTABLE
Esther obtained favour in the sight of all them that looked upon her. (2:15)

Who knoweth whether thou art come to the kingdom for such a time as this? (4:14)

UNIQUE AND UNUSUAL
God's name is never mentioned in the book of Esther. Neither is prayer, though Esther asks her fellow Jews to fast for her before she approaches the king (4:16).

SO WHAT?
When we find ourselves in bad situations, it may be for the same reason Esther did—to accomplish something good.

JOB

AUTHOR
Not stated.

DATE
Unclear, but many believe Job is one of the oldest stories in the Bible, perhaps from approximately 2000 BC.

IN TEN WORDS OR LESS
God allows human suffering for His own purposes.

DETAILS, PLEASE

Head of a large family, Job is a wealthy farmer from a place called Uz. He's "perfect and upright" (1:1)—so much so, that God calls Satan's attention to him. The devil, unimpressed, asks and receives God's permission to attack Job's possessions—and wipes out thousands of sheep, camels, oxen, donkeys, and worst of all, Job's ten children. Despite Satan's attack, Job keeps his faith. Satan then receives God's permission to attack Job's health—but in spite of terrible physical suffering, Job refuses to "curse God, and die" as his wife suggests (2:9). Before long, though, Job begins to question why God would allow him—a good man—to suffer so severely. Job's suffering is worsened by the arrival of four "friends" who begin to accuse him of causing his own trouble by secret sin. "Is not thy wickedness great?" asks Eliphaz the Temanite (22:5). In the end, God Himself speaks, vindicating Job before his friends and also addressing the overarching issue of human suffering. God doesn't explain Job's suffering but asks a series of questions that shows His vast knowledge—implying that Job should simply trust God's way. And Job does, telling God, "I know that thou canst do every thing" (42:2). By story's end, God has restored Job's health, possessions, and family, giving him ten more children.

QUOTABLE

Naked came I out of my mother's womb, and naked shall I return thither: the LORD gave, and the LORD hath taken away; blessed be the name of the LORD. (1:21)

Man that is born of a woman is of few days and full of trouble. (14:1)

Miserable comforters are ye all. (16:2)

I abhor myself, and repent in dust and ashes. (42:6)

UNIQUE AND UNUSUAL

The book of Job pictures Satan coming into God's presence (1:6). It also gives a clear Old Testament hint of Jesus' work when Job says, "I know that my redeemer liveth, and that he shall stand at the latter day upon the earth" (19:25).

SO WHAT?

Trouble isn't necessarily a sign of sin in a person's life. It may be something God allows to draw us closer to Him.

PSALMS

AUTHORS

Various, with nearly half attributed to King David. Other names noted include Solomon, Moses, Asaph, Ethan, and the sons of Korah. Many psalms don't mention an author.

Date
Approximately the 1400s BC (Moses' time) through the 500s BC (the time of the Jews' Babylonian exile).

In Ten Words or Less
Ancient Jewish songbook showcases prayers, praise—and complaints—to God.

Details, Please
Over several centuries, God led various individuals to compose emotionally charged poems—of which 150 were later compiled into the book we know as Psalms. Many of the psalms are described as "of David," meaning they could be *by*, *for*, or *about* Israel's great king. Highlights of the book include the "shepherd psalm" (23), which describes God as protector and provider; David's cry for forgiveness after his sin with Bathsheba (51); psalms of praise (100 is a powerful example); and the celebration of scripture found in Psalm 119, with almost all of the 176 verses making some reference to God's laws, statutes, commandments, precepts, word, and the like. Some psalms, called "imprecatory," call for God's judgment on enemies (see Psalms 69 and 109, for example). Many psalms express agony of spirit on the writer's part—but nearly every psalm returns to the theme of praise to God. That's the way the book of Psalms ends: "Let every thing that hath breath praise the Lord. Praise ye the Lord" (150:6).

Quotable
O Lord our Lord, how excellent is thy name in all the earth! (8:1)

The Lord is my shepherd; I shall not want. (23:1)

Create in me a clean heart, O God; and renew a right spirit within me. (51:10)

Thy word have I hid in mine heart, that I might not sin against thee. (119:11)

I will lift up mine eyes unto the hills, from whence cometh my help. My help cometh from the Lord. (121:1–2)

Behold, how good and how pleasant it is for brethren to dwell together in unity! (133:1)

Unique and Unusual
The book of Psalms is the Bible's longest, in terms of both number of chapters (150) and total word count. It contains the longest chapter in the Bible (Psalm 119, with 176 verses) and the shortest (Psalm 117, with 2 verses). Psalm 117 is also the midpoint of the Protestant Bible, with 594 chapters before it and 594 after.

So What?
The psalms run the gamut of human emotion—which is why so many people turn to them in times of both joy and sadness.

PROVERBS

AUTHORS
Primarily Solomon (1:1), with sections attributed to "the wise" (22:17), Agur (30:1), and King Lemuel (31:1). Little is known of the latter two.

DATE
Solomon reigned approximately 970–930 BC. The staff of King Hezekiah, who lived about two hundred years later, "copied out" the latter chapters of the book we have today (25:1).

IN TEN WORDS OR LESS
Pithy, memorable sayings encourage people to pursue wisdom.

DETAILS, PLEASE
Proverbs doesn't have a story line—it's simply a collection of practical tips for living. Mainly from the pen of King Solomon, the wisest human being ever (in 1 Kings 3:12 God said, "I have given thee a wise and an understanding heart; so that there was none like thee before thee, neither after thee shall any arise like unto thee"), the proverbs speak to issues such as work, money, sex, temptation, drinking, laziness, discipline, and child rearing. Underlying each proverb is the truth that "the fear of the LORD is the beginning of knowledge" (1:7).

QUOTABLE
Trust in the LORD with all thine heart; and lean not unto thine own understanding. (3:5)

Go to the ant, thou sluggard; consider her ways, and be wise. (6:6)

A wise son maketh a glad father: but a foolish son is the heaviness of his mother. (10:1)

As a jewel of gold in a swine's snout, so is a fair woman which is without discretion. (11:22)

He that spareth his rod hateth his son: but he that loveth him chasteneth him betimes. (13:24)

A soft answer turneth away wrath: but grievous words stir up anger. (15:1)

Commit thy works unto the LORD, and thy thoughts shall be established. (16:3)

Even a fool, when he holdeth his peace, is counted wise. (17:28)

The name of the LORD is a strong tower: the righteous runneth into it, and is safe. (18:10)

Wine is a mocker, strong drink is raging. (20:1)

A good name is rather to be chosen than great riches. (22:1)
Answer not a fool according to his folly, lest thou also be like unto him. (26:4)

Faithful are the wounds of a friend. (27:6)

Unique and Unusual
The final chapter of Proverbs includes a long poem in praise of wives, rather unusual for that time and culture.

So What?
Wisdom, as Proverbs 4:7 indicates, "is the principal thing. . .with all thy getting get understanding." If you need help with that, just ask God (James 1:5).

Ecclesiastes

Author
Not stated but probably Solomon. The author is identified as "the son of David" (1:1) and "king over Israel in Jerusalem" (1:12) and says he had "more wisdom than all they that have been before me" (1:16).

Date
900s BC.

In Ten Words or Less
Apart from God, life is empty and unsatisfying.

Details, Please
A king pursues the things of this world, only to find them unfulfilling. Learning, pleasure, work, laughter—"all is vanity" (1:2). The king also laments the inequities of life: People live, work hard, and die, only to leave their belongings to someone else; the wicked prosper over the righteous; the poor are oppressed. Nevertheless, the king realizes "the conclusion of the whole matter: Fear God, and keep his commandments: for this is the whole duty of man" (12:13).

Quotable
To every thing there is a season, and a time to every purpose under the heaven. (3:1)

Remember now thy Creator in the days of thy youth. (12:1)

Unique and Unusual
The book's generally negative tone makes some readers wonder if Solomon wrote it late in life, after his hundreds of wives led him to stray from God.

So What?
Life doesn't always make sense. . .but there's still a God who understands.

Song of Solomon

Author
Solomon (1:1), though some wonder if the song "of Solomon" is like the psalms "of David"—which could mean they are *by, for,* or *about* him.

Date
Solomon ruled around 970–930 BC.

In Ten Words or Less
Married love is a beautiful thing worth celebrating.

Details, Please
A dark-skinned beauty is marrying the king, and both are thrilled. "Behold, thou art fair, my love; behold, thou art fair; thou hast doves' eyes," he tells her (1:15). "Behold, thou art fair, my beloved, yea, pleasant: also our bed is green," she responds (1:16). Through eight chapters and 117 verses, the two lovers admire each other's physical beauty, expressing their love and devotion.

Quotable
Let him kiss me with the kisses of his mouth: for thy love is better than wine. (1:2)

He brought me to the banqueting house, and his banner over me was love. (2:4)

Many waters cannot quench love, neither can the floods drown it. (8:7)

Unique and Unusual
Like the book of Esther, Song of Solomon never mentions the name "God."

So What?
God made marriage for the husband and wife's enjoyment—and that marital love can be a picture of God's joy in His people.

Isaiah

Author
Isaiah, son of Amoz (1:1).

Date
Around 740–700 BC, starting "in the year that king Uzziah died" (6:1).

In Ten Words or Less
A coming Messiah will save people from their sins.

Details, Please
Like most prophets, Isaiah announced the bad news of punishment for sin. But he also described a coming Messiah who would be "wounded for our transgressions. . .bruised for our iniquities. . .and with his stripes we are healed" (53:5). Called to the ministry through a stunning vision of God in heaven (chapter 6), Isaiah wrote a book that some call "the fifth Gospel" for its predictions of the birth, life, and death of Jesus Christ some seven hundred years later. These prophecies of redemption balance the depressing promises of God's discipline against Judah and Jerusalem, which were overrun by Babylonian armies about a century later. Isaiah's prophecy ends with a long section (chapters 40–66) describing God's restoration of Israel, His promised salvation, and His eternal kingdom.

Quotable
Holy, holy, holy, is the LORD of hosts: the whole earth is full of his glory. (6:3)

Behold, a virgin shall conceive, and bear a son, and shall call his name Immanuel. (7:14)

For unto us a child is born, unto us a son is given: and the government shall be upon his shoulder: and his name shall be called Wonderful, Counsellor, The mighty God, The everlasting Father, The Prince of Peace. (9:6)
All we like sheep have gone astray; we have turned every one to his own way; and the LORD hath laid on him the iniquity of us all. (53:6)

Unique and Unusual
Isaiah had two children with strange, prophetic names. Shear-jashub (7:3) means "a remnant shall return," and Maher-shalal-hash-baz (8:3) means "haste to the spoil." Shear-jashub's name carried God's promise that exiled Jews would one day return home. Maher-shalal-hash-baz's name assured the king of Judah that his country's enemies would be handled by Assyrian armies.

So What?
Early in His ministry, Jesus said He fulfilled the prophecies of Isaiah: "The LORD hath anointed me to preach good tidings unto the meek; he hath sent me to bind up the brokenhearted, to proclaim liberty to the captives, and the opening of the prison to them that are bound; to proclaim the acceptable year of the LORD" (61:1–2). It's amazing how much God cares about us!

JEREMIAH

Author
Jeremiah (1:1), with the assistance of Baruch, a scribe (36:4).

DATE
Approximately 585 BC.

IN TEN WORDS OR LESS
After years of sinful behavior, Judah will be punished.

DETAILS, PLEASE
Called to the ministry as a boy (1:6), Jeremiah prophesies bad news to Judah: "Lo, I will bring a nation upon you from far, O house of Israel, saith the LORD" (5:15). Jeremiah is mocked for his prophecies, occasionally beaten, and imprisoned in a muddy well (chapter 38). But his words come true with the Babylonian invasion of chapter 52.

QUOTABLE
Behold, as the clay is in the potter's hand, so are ye in mine hand, O house of Israel. (18:6)

UNIQUE AND UNUSUAL
The book of Jeremiah that we read is apparently an expanded, second version of a destroyed first draft. King Jehoiakim, angry with Jeremiah for his dire prophecies, cut the scroll with a penknife and "cast it into the fire that was on the hearth" (36:23). At God's command, Jeremiah produced a second scroll with additional material (36:32).

SO WHAT?
Through Jeremiah, God gave Judah some forty years to repent. God "is longsuffering to us-ward, not willing that any should perish, but that all should come to repentance" (2 Peter 3:9).

LAMENTATIONS

AUTHOR
Not stated but traditionally attributed to Jeremiah.

DATE
Probably around 586 BC, shortly after the fall of Jerusalem to the Babylonians.

IN TEN WORDS OR LESS
A despairing poem about the destruction of Jerusalem.

DETAILS, PLEASE
After warning the southern Jewish nation to obey God, the prophet Jeremiah witnesses the punishment he'd threatened. Judah's "enemies prosper; for the LORD hath afflicted her for the multitude of her transgressions," writes Jeremiah; "her children are gone into captivity before the enemy" (1:5). The sight brings tears to Jeremiah's eyes ("Mine eye runneth down with water," 1:16) and provides his nickname, "the weeping prophet." Lamentations ends

with a plaintive cry: "Thou hast utterly rejected us; thou art very wroth against us" (5:22).

QUOTABLE
Turn thou us unto thee, O LORD, and we shall be turned; renew our days as of old. (5:21)

UNIQUE AND UNUSUAL
Though Lamentations doesn't indicate its author, Jeremiah is described in 2 Chronicles as a composer of laments (35:25).

SO WHAT?
God's punishment might seem severe, but as the book of Hebrews says, "No chastening for the present seemeth to be joyous, but grievous: nevertheless afterward it yieldeth the peaceable fruit of righteousness unto them which are exercised thereby" (12:11).

EZEKIEL

AUTHOR
Ezekiel, a priest (1:1–3).

DATE
Approximately the 590s–570s BC.

IN TEN WORDS OR LESS
Though Israel is in exile, the nation will be restored.

DETAILS, PLEASE
Ezekiel, an exiled Jew in Babylon, becomes God's spokesman to fellow exiles. He shares unusual (even bizarre) visions with the people, reminding them of the sin that led to their captivity but also offering hope of national restoration.

QUOTABLE
I have no pleasure in the death of him that dieth, saith the Lord GOD: wherefore turn yourselves, and live ye. (18:32)

UNIQUE AND UNUSUAL
Ezekiel's vision of a valley of dry bones is one of the Bible's strangest images: "I prophesied as I was commanded: and. . .there was a noise, and behold a shaking, and the bones came together. . . .The sinews and the flesh came up upon them, and the skin covered them above. . . . And the breath came into them, and they lived, and stood up upon their feet, an exceeding great army" (37:7–8, 10).

SO WHAT?
Ezekiel strongly teaches personal responsibility: "The soul that sinneth, it shall die. But if a man be just, and do that which is lawful and right. . .he shall surely live" (18:4–5, 9).

DANIEL

AUTHOR
Likely Daniel, though some question this. Chapters 7–12 are written in the first person ("I Daniel," 7:15), though the first six chapters are in the third person ("Then Daniel answered," 2:14).

DATE
The period of the Babylonian captivity, approximately 605–538 BC.

IN TEN WORDS OR LESS
Faithful to God in a challenging setting, Daniel is blessed.

DETAILS, PLEASE
As a young man, Daniel—along with three others to be known as Shadrach, Meshach, and Abednego—are taken from their home in Jerusalem to serve the king of Babylon. Daniel's God-given ability to interpret dreams endears him to King Nebuchadnezzar, whose vision of a huge statue, Daniel says, represents existing and future kingdoms. Shadrach, Meshach, and Abednego find trouble when they disobey an order to bow before a statue of Nebuchadnezzar; as punishment, they are thrown into a fiery furnace, where they are protected by an angelic being "like the Son of God" (3:25). The next Babylonian king, Belshazzar, throws a drinking party using cups stolen from the temple in Jerusalem; he literally sees "the writing on the wall," which Daniel interprets as the soon-to-come takeover of Babylon by the Medes. The Median king, Darius, keeps Daniel as an adviser but is tricked into passing a law designed by other jealous officials to hurt Daniel, who ends up in a den of lions. Once again, God protects His people; Daniel spending a night and replaced by the schemers, who are mauled by the hungry beasts. The final six chapters contain Daniel's prophetic visions, including that of "seventy weeks" of the end times.

QUOTABLE
Our God whom we serve is able to deliver us from the burning fiery furnace, and he will deliver us out of thine hand, O king. (3:17)

My God hath sent his angel, and hath shut the lions' mouths, that they have not hurt me. (6:22)

O my God. . .we do not present our supplications before thee for our righteousnesses, but for thy great mercies. (9:18)

UNIQUE AND UNUSUAL
The book was originally written in two languages: Hebrew (the introduction and most of the prophecies, chapter 1 and chapters 8–12) and Aramaic (the stories of chapters 2–7).

So What?

As the old song says, "Dare to be a Daniel." God will always take care of the people who "dare to stand alone. . .to have a purpose firm" for Him.

Hosea

Author

Probably Hosea himself, though the text is in both the first and the third person.

Date

Sometime between 750 (approximately when Hosea began ministering) and 722 BC (when Assyria overran Israel).

In Ten Words or Less

Prophet's marriage to prostitute reflects God's relationship with Israel.

Details, Please

God gives Hosea a strange command: "Take unto thee a wife of whoredoms" (1:2). The marriage pictures God's relationship to Israel—an honorable, loving husband paired with an unfaithful wife. Hosea marries an adulteress named Gomer and starts a family with her. When Gomer returns to her life of sin, Hosea—again picturing God's faithfulness—buys her back from the slave market. The book contains God's warnings for disobedience but also His promises of blessing for repentance.

Quotable

For they [Israel] have sown the wind, and they shall reap the whirlwind. (8:7)

Unique and Unusual

Gomer had three children—perhaps Hosea's but maybe not—each given a prophetic name. Son Jezreel was named for a massacre, daughter Lo-ruhamah's name meant "not loved," and son Lo-ammi's name meant "not my people."

So What?

God is faithful, even when His people aren't—and He's always ready to forgive. "I will heal their backsliding," God said through Hosea; "I will love them freely" (14:4).

Joel

Author

Joel, son of Pethuel (1:1). Little else is known about him.

Date

Unclear but possibly just before the Babylonian invasion of Judah in 586 BC.

In Ten Words or Less

Locust plague pictures God's judgment on His sinful people.

Details, Please

A devastating locust swarm invades the nation of Judah, but Joel indicates this natural disaster is nothing compared to the coming "great and very terrible" day of the Lord (2:11). God plans to judge His people for sin, but they still have time to repent. Obedience will bring both physical and spiritual renewal: "I will pour out my spirit upon all flesh," God says (2:28). When the Holy Spirit comes on Christian believers at Pentecost, the apostle Peter quotes this passage to explain what has happened (Acts 2:17).

Quotable

Whosoever shall call on the name of the LORD shall be delivered. (2:32)

Multitudes, multitudes in the valley of decision: for the day of the LORD is near in the valley of decision. (3:14)

Unique and Unusual

Unlike other prophets who condemned idolatry, injustice, or other specific sins of the Jewish people, Joel simply called for repentance without describing the sin committed.

So What?

Though God judges sin, He always offers a way out—in our time, through Jesus.

Amos

Author

Amos, a shepherd from Tekoa, near Bethlehem (1:1).

Date

Approximately the 760s BC.

In Ten Words or Less

Real religion isn't just ritual but treating people with justice.

Details, Please

An average guy—a lowly shepherd, actually—takes on the rich and powerful of Israelite society, condemning their idol worship, persecution of God's prophets, and cheating of the poor. Though God once rescued the people of Israel from slavery in Egypt, He is ready to send them into new bondage because of their sin. Amos sees visions that picture Israel's plight: a plumb line, indicating the people are not measuring up to God's standards, and a basket of ripe fruit, showing the nation is ripe for God's judgment.

Quotable
Prepare to meet thy God, O Israel. (4:12)

Seek good, and not evil, that ye may live. (5:14)

Let justice roll down as waters, and righteousness as a mighty stream. (5:24 ASV)

Unique and Unusual
A native of the southern Jewish kingdom of Judah, Amos was directed by God to prophesy in the northern Jewish nation of Israel.

So What?
How are you treating the people around you? In God's eyes, that's an indicator of your true spiritual condition. For a New Testament perspective, see James 2:14–18.

Obadiah

Author
Obadiah (1:1), perhaps a person by that name or an unnamed prophet for whom "Obadiah" (meaning "servant of God") is a title.

Date
Unclear but probably within thirty years after Babylon's invasion of Judah in 586 BC.

In Ten Words or Less
Edom will suffer for participating in Jerusalem's destruction.

Details, Please
Edom was a nation descended from Esau—twin brother of Jacob, the patriarch of Israel. The baby boys had struggled in their mother's womb (Genesis 25:21–26), and their conflict had continued over the centuries. After Edom took part in the Babylonian ransacking of Jerusalem, Obadiah passed down God's judgment: "For thy violence against thy brother Jacob shame shall cover thee, and thou shalt be cut off for ever" (1:10).

Quotable
Upon mount Zion shall be deliverance. (1:17)

Unique and Unusual
Obadiah is the Old Testament's shortest book—only one chapter and 21 verses.

So What?
Obadiah shows God's faithfulness to His people. This prophecy is a fulfillment of God's promise from generations earlier: "I will bless them that bless thee, and curse him that curseth thee" (Genesis 12:3).

JONAH

AUTHOR
Unclear; the story is Jonah's but is written in the third person.

DATE
Approximately 760 BC. Jonah prophesied during the reign of Israel's King Jeroboam II (see 2 Kings 14:23–25), who ruled from about 793 to 753 BC.

IN TEN WORDS OR LESS
Reluctant prophet, running from God, is swallowed by giant fish.

DETAILS, PLEASE
God tells Jonah to preach repentance in Nineveh, capital of the brutal Assyrian Empire. Jonah disobeys, sailing in the opposite direction—toward a rendezvous with literary immortality. A storm rocks Jonah's ship, and he spends three days in a giant fish's belly before deciding to obey God after all. When Jonah preaches, Nineveh repents—and God spares the city from the destruction He'd threatened. But the prejudiced Jonah pouts. The story ends with God proclaiming his concern even for vicious pagans.

QUOTABLE
I will pay that that I have vowed. Salvation is of the LORD. (2:9)

Should not I spare Nineveh, that great city, wherein are more than sixscore thousand persons that cannot discern between their right hand and their left hand? (4:11)

UNIQUE AND UNUSUAL
Jonah's prophecy didn't come true—because of Nineveh's repentance.

SO WHAT?
God loves *everyone*—even the enemies of His chosen people. As Romans 5:8 says, "God commendeth his love toward us, in that, while we were yet sinners, Christ died for us."

MICAH

AUTHOR
"The word of the LORD that came to Micah the Morasthite" (1:1). Micah either wrote the prophecies or dictated them to another.

DATE
Approximately 700 BC.

IN TEN WORDS OR LESS
Israel and Judah will suffer for their idolatry and injustice.

DETAILS, PLEASE

Micah chastises both the northern and southern Jewish nations for pursuing false gods and cheating the poor. The two nations will be devastated by invaders (the Assyrians), but God will preserve "the remnant of Israel" (2:12).

QUOTABLE

He hath shewed thee, O man, what is good; and what doth the LORD require of thee, but to do justly, and to love mercy, and to walk humbly with thy God? (6:8)

UNIQUE AND UNUSUAL

Centuries before Jesus' birth, Micah predicted the town where it would occur: "But thou, Bethlehem Ephratah, though thou be little among the thousands of Judah, yet out of thee shall he come forth unto me that is to be ruler in Israel" (5:2).

SO WHAT?

Micah shows how God's judgment is tempered by mercy. "Who is a God like unto thee, that pardoneth iniquity, and passeth by the transgression of the remnant of his heritage? he retaineth not his anger for ever, because he delighteth in mercy" (7:18).

NAHUM

AUTHOR

"The book of the vision of Nahum the Elkoshite" (1:1). Nahum either wrote the prophecies or dictated them to another.

DATE

Sometime between 663 and 612 BC.

IN TEN WORDS OR LESS

Powerful, wicked Nineveh will fall before God's judgment.

DETAILS, PLEASE

"Woe to the bloody city!" Nahum cries (3:1). Nineveh, capital of the brutal Assyrian Empire, has been targeted for judgment by God Himself, who will "make thee vile, and will set thee as a gazingstock" (3:6) for sins of idolatry and cruelty. Nahum's prophecy comes true when the Babylonian Empire overruns Nineveh in 612 BC.

QUOTABLE

The LORD is slow to anger, and great in power, and will not at all acquit the wicked. (1:3)

The LORD is good, a strong hold in the day of trouble; and he knoweth them that trust in him. (1:7)

Unique and Unusual
Nahum is a kind of Jonah, part 2. Though the city had once avoided God's judgment by taking Jonah's preaching to heart and repenting, now, more than a century later, it will experience the full consequence of its sins.

So What?
Even the most powerful city on earth is no match for God's strength. Neither is the biggest problem in our individual lives.

Habakkuk

Author
Habakkuk (1:1); nothing is known of his background.

Date
Approximately 600 BC.

In Ten Words or Less
Trust God even when He seems unresponsive or unfair.

Details, Please
In Judah, a prophet complains that God allows violence and injustice among His people. But Habakkuk is shocked to learn the Lord's plan for dealing with the problem: sending the "bitter and hasty" (1:6) Chaldeans to punish Judah. Habakkuk argues that the Chaldeans are far worse than the disobedient Jews, telling God, "Thou art of purer eyes than to behold evil" (1:13). The Lord, however, says He's only using the Chaldeans for His purposes and will in time punish them for their own sins. It's not Habakkuk's job to question God's ways: "The LORD is in his holy temple: let all the earth keep silence before him" (2:20). Habakkuk, like Job, ultimately submits to God's authority.

Quotable
The just shall live by his faith. (2:4)

I will joy in the God of my salvation. (3:18)

Unique and Unusual
The apostle Paul quotes Habakkuk 2:4 in his powerful gospel presentation in Romans 1.

So What?
Our world is much like Habakkuk's—full of violence and injustice—but God is still in control. Whether we sense it or not, He's working out His own purposes.

ZEPHANIAH

AUTHOR
Zephaniah (1:1).

DATE
Approximately 640–620 BC, during the reign of King Josiah (1:1).

IN TEN WORDS OR LESS
A coming "day of the Lord" promises heavy judgment.

DETAILS, PLEASE
Zephaniah begins with a jarring prophecy: "I will utterly consume all things from off the land," God declares in the book's second verse. People, animals, birds, and fish will all perish, victims of God's wrath over Judah's idolatry. Other nearby nations will be punished, as well, in "the fire of my jealousy" (3:8), but there is hope: In His mercy, God will one day restore a remnant of Israel that "shall not do iniquity, nor speak lies" (3:13).

QUOTABLE
The great day of the LORD is near. . .and hasteth greatly. (1:14)

The LORD thy God in the midst of thee is mighty; he will save, he will rejoice over thee with joy. (3:17)

UNIQUE AND UNUSUAL
Zephaniah gives more detail about himself than most of the minor prophets, identifying himself as a great-great-grandson of Hezekiah (1:1), probably the popular, godly king of Judah (2 Chronicles 29).

SO WHAT?
God gave the people of Judah fair warning of His judgment, just as He has done with us. For Christians, the coming "day of the Lord" carries no fear.

HAGGAI

AUTHOR
Haggai (1:1).

DATE
520 BC—a precise date because Haggai mentions "the second year of Darius the king" (1:1), which can be verified against Persian records.

IN TEN WORDS OR LESS
Jews returning from exile need to rebuild God's temple.

DETAILS, PLEASE

One of three "postexilic" prophets, Haggai encourages former Babylonian captives to restore the demolished temple in Jerusalem. The new world power, Persia, has allowed the people to return to Jerusalem, but they've become distracted with building their own comfortable homes. Through Haggai, God tells the people to rebuild the temple first in order to break a drought that's affecting the countryside.

QUOTABLE

Be strong, all ye people of the land, saith the LORD, and work: for I am with you, saith the LORD of hosts. (2:4)

UNIQUE AND UNUSUAL

Haggai seems to hint at the end-times tribulation and second coming of Christ when he quotes God as saying, "I will shake the heavens, and the earth, and the sea, and the dry land; and I will shake all nations, and the desire of all nations shall come" (2:6–7).

SO WHAT?

Priorities are important. When we put God first, He is more inclined to bless us.

ZECHARIAH

AUTHOR

Zechariah, son of Berechiah (1:1); some believe a second, unnamed writer contributed chapters 9–14.

DATE

Approximately 520–475 BC.

IN TEN WORDS OR LESS

Jewish exiles should rebuild their temple—and anticipate their Messiah.

DETAILS, PLEASE

Like Haggai, another postexilic prophet, Zechariah urges Jewish people to rebuild the Jerusalem temple. He also gives several prophecies of the coming Messiah, including an end-times vision of a final battle over Jerusalem, when "the LORD [shall] go forth, and fight against those nations. . . . And his feet shall stand in that day upon the mount of Olives. . . . And the LORD shall be king over all the earth" (14:3–4, 9).

QUOTABLE

Turn ye unto me, saith the LORD of hosts, and I will turn unto you. (1:3)

UNIQUE AND UNUSUAL

Zechariah's prophecy of the Messiah riding a donkey into Jerusalem (9:9) was fulfilled to the letter in Jesus' "triumphal entry" (Matthew 21:1–11). The prophecy "They shall look upon me whom they have pierced" (12:10) refers to the Roman soldiers' spearing of Christ after the crucifixion (John 19:34).

So What?
Knowing that many of Zechariah's specific prophecies were fulfilled in Jesus, we can trust that his other predictions—of the end times—will come true, too.

MALACHI

Author
Malachi (1:1), meaning "my messenger." No other details are given.

Date
Approximately 450 BC.

In Ten Words or Less
The Jews have become careless in their attitude toward God.

Details, Please
Prophesying a century after the return from exile, Malachi chastises the Jews for offering "lame and sick" sacrifices (1:8); for divorcing their wives to marry pagan women (2:11, 14); and for failing to pay tithes for the temple (3:8). The Lord was angry with the attitude "It is vain to serve God" (3:14), but He promised to bless the obedient: "Unto you that fear my name shall the Sun of righteousness arise with healing in his wings" (4:2).

Quotable
Return unto me, and I will return unto you, saith the LORD of hosts. (3:7)

Unique and Unusual
Malachi, the last book of the Old Testament, contains the final word from God for some four hundred years, until the appearance of John the Baptist and Jesus, the Messiah, as prophesied in Malachi 3:1: "I will send my messenger, and he shall prepare the way before me, and the Lord, whom ye seek, shall suddenly come to his temple."

So What?
God doesn't want empty religious rituals—He wants people to worship Him "in spirit and in truth" (John 4:24).

MATTHEW

Author
Not stated but traditionally attributed to Matthew, a tax collector (9:9). Matthew is also known as "Levi" (Mark 2:14).

Date
Approximately AD 70, when Romans destroyed the temple in Jerusalem.

In Ten Words or Less
Jesus fulfills the Old Testament prophecies of a coming Messiah.

Details, Please
The first of the four *Gospels* (meaning "good news"), the book of Matthew ties what follows in the New Testament to what came before in the Old. The book, written primarily to a Jewish audience, uses numerous Old Testament references to prove that Jesus is the promised Messiah the Jews have been anticipating for centuries. Beginning with a genealogy that shows Jesus' ancestry through King David and the patriarch Abraham, Matthew then details the angelic announcement of Jesus' conception and the visit of the "wise men" with their gifts of gold, frankincense, and myrrh. Matthew introduces the character of John the Baptist, relative and forerunner of Jesus, and describes the calling of key disciples Peter, Andrew, James, and John. Jesus' teachings are emphasized, with long passages covering His Sermon on the Mount (chapters 5–7), including the Beatitudes ("Blessed are they...") and the Lord's Prayer ("Our Father, which art in heaven..."). As with all four Gospels, Matthew also details the death, burial, and resurrection of Jesus and is the only biographer of Jesus to mention several miracles—the tearing of the temple curtain, an earthquake, the breaking open of tombs, and the raising to life of dead saints—that occurred during that time (27:50–54).

Quotable
She shall bring forth a son, and thou shalt call his name JESUS: for he shall save his people from their sins. (1:21)

Ye are the salt of the earth.... Ye are the light of the world. (5:13–14)

Love your enemies, bless them that curse you, do good to them that hate you, and pray for them which despitefully use you, and persecute you. (5:44)

Judge not, that ye be not judged. (7:1)

Ask, and it shall be given you; seek, and ye shall find; knock, and it shall be opened unto you. (7:7)

Go ye therefore, and teach all nations, baptizing them in the name of the Father, and of the Son, and of the Holy Ghost. (28:19)

Unique and Unusual
Matthew is the only Gospel to use the terms "church" and "kingdom of heaven."

So What?
As Messiah, Jesus is also King—and worthy of our worship.

MARK

AUTHOR
Not stated but traditionally attributed to John Mark, a missionary companion of Paul and Barnabas (Acts 12:25) and an associate of the apostle Peter (1 Peter 5:13).

DATE
Probably AD 60s, during the Roman persecution of Christians.

IN TEN WORDS OR LESS
Jesus is God's Son, a suffering servant of all people.

DETAILS, PLEASE
The second of the four Gospels is believed by most to be the first one written. The book of Mark is the briefest and most active of the four biographies of Jesus, the majority of which is repeated in the Gospels of Matthew and Luke. Mark addresses a Gentile audience, portraying Jesus as a man of action, divinely capable of healing the sick, controlling nature, and battling the powers of Satan. Mark's theme of the suffering servant comes through in his narratives of Jesus' interaction with hostile doubters—the Jewish leaders, who want to kill Him (9:31); His neighbors, who take offense at Him (6:3); and even His own family members, who think He's crazy (3:21). The abasement of Jesus pictures what His disciples should pursue: "Whosoever will be great among you, shall be your minister: and whosoever of you will be the chiefest, shall be servant of all. For even the Son of man came not to be ministered unto, but to minister, and to give his life a ransom for many" (10:43–45).

QUOTABLE
Come ye after me, and I will make you to become fishers of men. (1:17)

Suffer the little children to come unto me, and forbid them not: for of such is the kingdom of God. (10:14)

It is easier for a camel to go through the eye of a needle, than for a rich man to enter into the kingdom of God. (10:25)

Render to Caesar the things that are Caesar's, and to God the things that are God's. (12:17)

Watch ye and pray, lest ye enter into temptation. The spirit truly is ready, but the flesh is weak. (14:38)

UNIQUE AND UNUSUAL
Many believe an unnamed spectator at Jesus' arrest, mentioned in Mark's Gospel, was Mark himself: "And there followed him a certain young man, having a linen cloth cast about his naked body; and the young men laid hold on him: and he left the linen cloth, and fled from them naked" (14:51–52).

So What?
Suffering and loss aren't necessarily bad things—in fact, for Christians, they're the pathway to real life (8:35).

Luke

Author
Not stated but traditionally attributed to Luke, a Gentile physician (Colossians 4:14) and a missionary companion of the apostle Paul (2 Timothy 4:11).

Date
Possibly the AD 70s–80s, as the gospel was spreading throughout the Roman Empire.

In Ten Words or Less
Jesus is Savior of all people, whether Jew or Gentile.

Details, Please
Luke's Gospel is addressed to a man named Theophilus (1:3), "to set forth in order a declaration of those things which are most surely believed among us" about Jesus Christ (1:1). It's unclear who Theophilus was, though some believe he may have been a Roman official—and Luke's book is the least Jewish and most universal of the four Gospels. Luke traces Jesus' genealogy beyond Abraham, the patriarch of the Jews, all the way back to Adam, "the son of God" (3:38), common ancestor of everyone. Luke also shows Jesus' compassion for all people: Roman soldiers (7:1–10), widows (7:11–17), the "sinful" (7:36–50), the chronically ill (8:43–48), lepers (17:11–19), and many others—including a criminal condemned to die on a cross beside Jesus (23:40–43). As with all the Gospels, Luke shows Jesus' resurrection, adding detailed accounts of His appearances to two believers on the Emmaus road and the remaining eleven disciples. As the Gospel ends, Jesus is ascending into heaven—setting the stage for a sequel of sorts, Luke's book of Acts.

Quotable
For where your treasure is, there will your heart be also. (12:34)

I say unto you, that likewise joy shall be in heaven over one sinner that repenteth, more than over ninety and nine just persons, which need no repentance. (15:7)
Whosoever shall seek to save his life shall lose it; and whosoever shall lose his life shall preserve it. (17:33)

Whosoever shall not receive the kingdom of God as a little child shall in no wise enter therein. (18:17)

For the Son of man is come to seek and to save that which was lost. (19:10)

Unique and Unusual

Luke is the only Gospel to share Jesus' stories ("parables") of the good Samaritan (10:25–37), the prodigal son (15:11–32), and the rich man and Lazarus (16:19–31). Luke is also the only Gospel to detail Jesus' actual birth and words He spoke in childhood (both in chapter 2).

So What?

It doesn't matter who you are, where you come from, or what you've done—Jesus came to seek and to save you.

John

Author

Not stated but traditionally attributed to John, the "disciple whom Jesus loved" (John 21:7), brother of James and son of Zebedee (Matthew 4:21).

Date

Around the AD 90s, as the last Gospel written.

In Ten Words or Less

Jesus is God Himself, the only Savior of the world.

Details, Please

While the books of Matthew, Mark, and Luke have many similarities (they're called the "synoptic Gospels," meaning they take a common view), the book of John stands alone. The fourth Gospel downplays Jesus' parables (none are recorded) and miracles (only seven are featured). Instead, John provides more extensive treatments of Jesus' reasons for coming to earth ("I am come that they might have life, and that they might have it more abundantly," 10:10); His intimate relationship with God the Father ("I and my Father are one," 10:30); and His own feelings toward the job He had come to do ("Father, the hour is come; glorify thy Son, that thy Son also may glorify thee: as thou hast given him power over all flesh, that he should give eternal life to as many as thou hast given him," 17:1–2). John also gives special emphasis to Jesus' patient treatment of the disciples Thomas, who doubted the resurrection (20:24–29), and Peter, who had denied the Lord (21:15–23).

Quotable

In the beginning was the Word, and the Word was with God, and the Word was God. (1:1)

For God so loved the world, that he gave his only begotten Son, that whosoever believeth in him should not perish, but have everlasting life. (3:16)

I am the bread of life. (6:35)

I am the good shepherd: the good shepherd giveth his life for the sheep. (10:11)

I am the way, the truth, and the life: no man cometh unto the Father, but by me. (14:6)

UNIQUE AND UNUSUAL

Jesus' very first miracle, His changing of water into wine at a wedding in Cana, is recorded only in John's Gospel (2:1–12). So is His raising of Lazarus from the dead (11:1–44), His healing of a man born blind (9:1–38), and His long-distance healing of a nobleman's son (4:46–54). John is also the only Gospel to mention Nicodemus, who heard Jesus' teaching that "ye must be born again" (3:7).

SO WHAT?

"These are written, that ye might believe that Jesus is the Christ, the Son of God; and that believing ye might have life through his name" (20:31).

ACTS

AUTHOR

Not stated but traditionally attributed to Luke, a Gentile physician (Colossians 4:14), a missionary companion of the apostle Paul (2 Timothy 4:11), and the author of the Gospel of Luke.

DATE

Covering events of the AD 30s–60s, Acts was probably written sometime between AD 62 and 80.

IN TEN WORDS OR LESS

The Holy Spirit's arrival heralds the beginning of Christian church.

DETAILS, PLEASE

Officially called "Acts of the Apostles," the book of Acts is a bridge between the story of Jesus in the Gospels and the life of the church in the letters that follow. Luke begins with Jesus' ascension into heaven after forty days of post-resurrection activity, "speaking of the things pertaining to the kingdom of God" (1:3). Ten days later, God sends the Holy Spirit on the festival day of Pentecost—and the church is born. Through the Spirit, the disciples are empowered to preach boldly about Jesus, and three thousand people become Christians that day. Jewish leaders, fearing the new movement called "this way" (9:2), begin persecuting believers, who scatter to other areas and spread the gospel through much of the known world. The ultimate persecutor, Saul, becomes a Christian himself after meeting the brightly shining, heavenly Jesus on the road to Damascus. Saul, later called Paul, ultimately joins Peter and other Christian leaders in preaching, working miracles, and strengthening the fledgling church.

QUOTABLE

Ye men of Galilee, why stand ye gazing up into heaven? this same Jesus, which is taken up from you into heaven, shall so come in like manner as ye have seen him go into heaven. (1:11)

Repent, and be baptized every one of you in the name of Jesus Christ for the remission of sins, and ye shall receive the gift of the Holy Ghost. (2:38)

Neither is there salvation in any other: for there is none other name under heaven given among men, whereby we must be saved. (4:12)

Saul, Saul, why persecutest thou me? (9:4)

UNIQUE AND UNUSUAL
Acts tells of the first Christian martyr, Stephen, stoned to death for blaming Jewish leaders for the death of Jesus (chapter 7). Acts also depicts the gospel's transition from a purely Jewish message to one for all people (9:15; 10:45) and the beginning of the Christian missionary movement (chapter 13).

SO WHAT?
Christians today are driven by the same force that Acts describes: "Ye shall receive power, after that the Holy Ghost is come upon you" (1:8).

ROMANS

AUTHOR
The apostle Paul (1:1), with the secretarial assistance of Tertius (16:22).

DATE
Approximately AD 57, near the conclusion of Paul's third missionary journey.

IN TEN WORDS OR LESS
Sinners are saved only by faith in Jesus Christ.

DETAILS, PLEASE
Some call Romans a "theology textbook" for its thorough explanation of the Christian life. Paul begins by describing God's righteous anger against human sin (chapters 1–2), noting that everyone falls short of God's standard (3:23). But God Himself provides the only way to overcome that sin, "the righteousness of God which is by faith of Jesus Christ unto all and upon all them that believe" (3:22). Being justified (made right) through faith in Jesus, we can consider ourselves "to be dead indeed unto sin, but alive unto God through Jesus Christ our Lord" (6:11). God's Spirit will "quicken" (give life to, 8:11) all who believe in Jesus, allowing us to "present [our] bodies a living sacrifice, holy, acceptable unto God" (12:1). It is possible, with God's help, to "be not overcome of evil, but [to] overcome evil with good" (12:21).

QUOTABLE
All have sinned, and come short of the glory of God. (3:23)

God commendeth his love toward us, in that, while we were yet sinners, Christ died for us. (5:8)

The wages of sin is death; but the gift of God is eternal life through Jesus Christ our Lord. (6:23)

O wretched man that I am! who shall deliver me from the body of this death? I thank God through Jesus Christ our Lord. (7:24–25)
We know that all things work together for good to them that love God, to them who are the called according to his purpose. (8:28)

Owe no man any thing, but to love one another: for he that loveth another hath fulfilled the law. (13:8)

Love worketh no ill to his neighbour: therefore love is the fulfilling of the law. (13:10)

Unique and Unusual
Unlike Paul's other letters to churches, Romans was addressed to a congregation he'd never met. The great missionary was hoping to see the Roman Christians personally while traveling westward to Spain (15:23–24). It's unclear if Paul ever actually reached Spain or if he was executed in Rome after the end of the book of Acts.

So What?
In Paul's own words, "Therefore being justified by faith, we have peace with God through our Lord Jesus Christ" (5:1).

1 Corinthians

Author
The apostle Paul, with the assistance of Sosthenes (1:1).

Date
Approximately AD 55–57.

In Ten Words or Less
An apostle tackles sin problems in the church at Corinth.

Details, Please
Paul had helped found the church in Corinth (Acts 18) but then moved on to other mission fields. While in Ephesus, he learns of serious problems in the Corinthian congregation and writes a long letter to address those issues. For those arguing over who should lead the church, Paul urges "that ye be perfectly joined together in the same mind and in the same judgment" (1:10). For a man involved in an immoral relationship with his stepmother, Paul commands, "Put away from among yourselves that wicked person" (5:13). For those church

members filing lawsuits against others, Paul warns, "Know ye not that the unrighteous shall not inherit the kingdom of God?" (6:9). The apostle also teaches on marriage, Christian liberty, the Lord's Supper, spiritual gifts, and the resurrection of the dead. In the famous thirteenth chapter of 1 Corinthians, Paul describes the "more excellent way" (12:31): that of charity, or love.

QUOTABLE

For the preaching of the cross is to them that perish foolishness; but unto us which are saved it is the power of God. (1:18)

The foolishness of God is wiser than men; and the weakness of God is stronger than men. (1:25)

For other foundation can no man lay than that is laid, which is Jesus Christ. (3:11)

Take heed lest by any means this liberty of yours become a stumblingblock to them that are weak. (8:9)

I am made all things to all men, that I might by all means save some. (9:22)

For as often as ye eat this bread, and drink this cup, ye do shew the Lord's death till he come. (11:26)

Though I speak with the tongues of men and of angels, and have not charity, I am become as sounding brass, or a tinkling cymbal. (13:1)

UNIQUE AND UNUSUAL

Refuting opponents who questioned his apostleship, Paul insists that he is as much an apostle as Jesus' original disciples. "Am I am not an apostle?" he asks in 1 Corinthians 9:1. "Have I not seen Jesus Christ our Lord?"

SO WHAT?

Church problems are nothing new—neither is the way to correct them. Personal purity, self-discipline, and love for others are vital to a congregation's success.

2 CORINTHIANS

AUTHOR

The apostle Paul, with Timothy's assistance (1:1).

DATE

Approximately AD 55–57, shortly after the writing of 1 Corinthians.

IN TEN WORDS OR LESS

Paul defends his ministry to the troubled Corinthian church.

DETAILS, PLEASE

Corinthian believers had apparently addressed some of the problems Paul's first letter mentioned—though there were still troublemakers who questioned his authority. He was forced to "speak foolishly" (11:21), boasting of hardships he'd faced serving Jesus: "in labours more abundant, in stripes above measure, in prisons more frequent, in deaths oft" (11:23). Paul even suffered a "thorn in the flesh" (12:7), which God refused to take away, telling him instead, "My grace is sufficient for thee: for my strength is made perfect in weakness" (12:9). His parting warning: "Examine yourselves, whether ye be in the faith; prove your own selves" (13:5).

QUOTABLE

For he hath made him to be sin for us, who knew no sin; that we might be made the righteousness of God in him. (5:21)

UNIQUE AND UNUSUAL

Paul never identifies his "thorn in the flesh," though some speculate it may have been bad eyesight, temptations, even physical unattractiveness.

SO WHAT?

Christians should respect authority—whether in the church, the home, or society at large.

GALATIANS

AUTHOR

The apostle Paul (1:1).

DATE

Perhaps around AD 49, as one of Paul's earliest letters.

IN TEN WORDS OR LESS

Christians are free from restrictive Jewish laws.

DETAILS, PLEASE

Writing to several regional churches, Paul can only "marvel" (1:6) that Galatian Christians have turned from their freedom in Jesus back to the rules of Old Testament Judaism. Some people tried to compel Christians "to live as do the Jews" (2:14), an error even the apostle Peter made (2:11–13). Paul argued strongly "that no man is justified by the law in the sight of God. . .for, The just shall live by faith" (3:11).

QUOTABLE

O foolish Galatians, who hath bewitched you? (3:1)

The fruit of the Spirit is love, joy, peace, longsuffering, gentleness, goodness, faith, meekness, temperance: against such there is no law. (5:22–23)

UNIQUE AND UNUSUAL
One of Paul's closing comments, "Ye see how large a letter I have written unto you with mine own hand" (6:11), makes some believe that poor eyesight was the apostle's "thorn in the flesh" (2 Corinthians 12:7).

SO WHAT?
Old Testament rules don't control Christians' lives—but God's Spirit should: "Walk in the Spirit, and ye shall not fulfil the lust of the flesh" (5:16).

EPHESIANS

AUTHOR
The apostle Paul (1:1).

DATE
Around AD 62, toward the end of Paul's life.

IN TEN WORDS OR LESS
Christians are all members of Jesus' "body," the church.

DETAILS, PLEASE
Paul had started the church in Ephesus (Acts 19) and now explains in detail the church members' relationship to Jesus Christ—so that they "may grow up into him in all things, which is the head, even Christ" (4:15). Through Jesus, God has reconciled both Jews and Gentiles to Himself (2:11–18). This new life should result in pure, honest living in the church and in the home (chapters 4–6).

QUOTABLE
By grace are ye saved through faith; and that not of yourselves: it is the gift of God: not of works, lest any man should boast. (2:8–9)

Put on the whole armour of God, that ye may be able to stand against the wiles of the devil. (6:11)

UNIQUE AND UNUSUAL
Paul tells servants (slaves, in today's language) to "be obedient to them that are your masters" (6:5). Why? Because God will reward such behavior (6:8).

SO WHAT?
"In him [Jesus] you too are being built together to become a dwelling in which God lives by his Spirit" (2:22 NIV).

PHILIPPIANS

AUTHOR
The apostle Paul, along with Timothy (1:1).

DATE
Probably the early 60s AD

IN TEN WORDS OR LESS
"Friendship letter" between the apostle Paul and a beloved church.

DETAILS, PLEASE
With sixteen references to "joy" and "rejoicing," Philippians is one of the apostle Paul's most upbeat letters—even though he wrote it in "bonds" (1:13). Paul thanks the church at Philippi for its support (1:5) and encourages its people to "rejoice in the Lord alway: and again I say, Rejoice" (4:4).

QUOTABLE
For to me to live is Christ, and to die is gain. (1:21)

I press toward the mark for the prize of the high calling of God in Christ Jesus. (3:14)

Be careful for nothing; but in every thing by prayer and supplication with thanksgiving let your requests be made known unto God. (4:6)

UNIQUE AND UNUSUAL
Though unity is a common theme in Paul's letters, he singles out two Philippian women, Euodias and Syntyche, pleading that they "be of the same mind in the Lord" (4:2).

SO WHAT?
When we live in the joy of the Lord, "the peace of God, which passeth all understanding, shall keep your hearts and minds through Christ Jesus" (4:7).

COLOSSIANS

AUTHOR
The apostle Paul, along with Timothy (1:1).

DATE
Probably the early 60s AD

IN TEN WORDS OR LESS
Jesus Christ is supreme—over everyone and everything.

DETAILS, PLEASE
False teaching ("enticing words," 2:4) had infiltrated the church at Colosse, apparently causing some people to add unnecessary and unhelpful elements to their Christian faith. Paul sent this letter to remind Christians of the superiority of Jesus over Jewish rules and regulations (2:16), angels (2:18), and anything else. Jesus is "the image of the invisible God, the firstborn of every creature" (1:15).

Quotable

For this cause we also, since the day we heard it, do not cease to pray for you. (1:9)

Set your affection on things above, not on things on the earth. (3:2)

Let the peace of God rule in your hearts, to the which also ye are called in one body; and be ye thankful. (3:15)

Unique and Unusual

Paul mentions a letter to Laodicea (4:16) that apparently did not make the cut as New Testament scripture.

So What?

"Beware lest any man spoil you through philosophy and vain deceit, after the tradition of men. . .and not after Christ" (2:8).

1 Thessalonians

Author

The apostle Paul, along with Silvanus (Silas) and Timothy (1:1).

Date

The early 50s AD—perhaps Paul's earliest letter.

In Ten Words or Less

Jesus will return to gather His followers to Him.

Details, Please

In this letter to another church he helped found (see Acts 17), Paul teaches on the second coming of Christ, apparently an issue of some concern to the Thessalonians. Paul describes *how* Jesus will return but doesn't say exactly *when*. The important thing, in his words, is "that ye would walk worthy of God, who hath called you unto his kingdom and glory" (2:12).

Quotable

For the Lord himself shall descend from heaven with a shout, with the voice of the archangel, and with the trump of God: and the dead in Christ shall rise first. (4:16)

The day of the Lord so cometh as a thief in the night. (5:2)

Unique and Unusual

First Thessalonians contains two of the Bible's shortest verses: "Rejoice evermore" (5:16) and "Pray without ceasing" (5:17).

So What?
The Thessalonians were told to live right in view of Jesus' coming return. With the passage of two thousand years, don't you think it's more important for us today?

2 Thessalonians

Author
The apostle Paul, along with Silvanus (Silas) and Timothy (1:1).

Date
The early 50s AD—perhaps Paul's second-oldest letter.

In Ten Words or Less
Christians should work until Jesus returns.

Details, Please
Shortly after writing 1 Thessalonians, Paul dictates a follow-up. Apparently, a letter falsely claiming to be from Paul had left the Thessalonians "shaken in mind. . .troubled" (2:2) at the thought that Jesus had already returned. Paul assures them that the event is still future—and urges everyone to live positive and productive lives until the second coming. "If any would not work," Paul commands those who have dropped out in anticipation of Jesus' return, "neither should he eat" (3:10).

Quotable
You who are troubled rest with us, when the Lord Jesus shall be revealed from heaven with his mighty angels. (1:7)

Brethren, be not weary in well doing. (3:13)

Unique and Unusual
The fact that Paul dictated this letter is clear from his comment "The salutation of Paul with mine own hand. . .so I write" (3:17).

So What?
As with all of the Christian life, balance is key: We should always look forward to Jesus' return, but we should also be busy doing good while we're here on earth.

1 Timothy

Author
The apostle Paul (1:1).

Date
Approximately AD 63.

In Ten Words or Less
Pastors are taught how to conduct their lives and churches.

Details, Please
The first of three "pastoral epistles," 1 Timothy contains the aging apostle Paul's insights for a new generation of church leaders. Timothy had often worked alongside Paul but was now pastoring in Ephesus (1:3). Paul warned him against legalism and false teaching (chapter 1), listed the qualifications for pastors and deacons (chapter 3), and described the behavior of a "good minister of Jesus Christ" (4:6) in the final three chapters.

Quotable
Christ Jesus came into the world to save sinners; of whom I am chief. (1:15)

This is a true saying, If a man desire the office of a bishop, he desireth a good work. (3:1)

Unique and Unusual
First Timothy seems to command good pay for pastors: "Let the elders that rule well be counted worthy of double honour. . . . The labourer is worthy of his reward" (5:17–18).

So What?
Though 1 Timothy is a letter to a pastor, Paul's teaching "that thou mayest know how thou oughtest to behave thyself in the house of God" (3:15) can speak to the rest of us, too.

2 Timothy

Author
The apostle Paul (1:1).

Date
Probably the mid-60s AD.

In Ten Words or Less
The apostle Paul's final words to a beloved coworker.

Details, Please
Second Timothy may be the last known letter of Paul. Addressed to "Timothy, my dearly beloved son" (1:2), the book warns the young pastor against false teaching and urges him to live a life of purity before his congregation. Timothy should expect trouble ("All that will live godly in Christ Jesus shall suffer persecution," 3:12), but God will be faithful ("The Lord shall deliver me from every evil work, and will preserve me unto his heavenly kingdom," 4:18). Paul begs Timothy to join him as quickly as possible, as "the time of my departure is at hand" (4:6).

QUOTABLE
Thou therefore endure hardness, as a good soldier of Jesus Christ. (2:3)

UNIQUE AND UNUSUAL
Paul tells where the Bible comes from in 2 Timothy: "All scripture is given by inspiration of God" (3:16). The idea of the word *inspiration* is "breathed out."

SO WHAT?
We should all live life in such a way that we can say, like Paul, "I have fought a good fight, I have finished my course, I have kept the faith" (4:7).

TITUS

AUTHOR
The apostle Paul (1:1).

DATE
Approximately AD 63.

IN TEN WORDS OR LESS
Church leaders are instructed on their lives and teaching.

DETAILS, PLEASE
On the Mediterranean island of Crete, Paul left Titus to "set in order the things that are wanting, and ordain elders" (1:5) for the fledgling church. Known for their poor behavior (see "Unique and Unusual" below), the people of Crete needed the kind of church leader who holds fast to "the faithful word as he hath been taught, that he may be able by sound doctrine both to exhort and to convince the gainsayers" (1:9).

QUOTABLE
Not by works of righteousness which we have done, but according to his mercy he saved us, by the washing of regeneration, and renewing of the Holy Ghost. (3:5)

UNIQUE AND UNUSUAL
Paul quotes a Cretan philosopher in this letter: "One of themselves, even a prophet of their own, said, The Cretians are alway liars, evil beasts, slow bellies" (1:12). The quotation is from Epimenides, of the sixth century BC.

SO WHAT?
Though church leaders are held to a high standard, so are the people in the pews. What's good for the pastor is good for everyone else.

PHILEMON

AUTHOR
The apostle Paul (1:1).

DATE
Probably around AD 63, when Paul was imprisoned in Rome.

IN TEN WORDS OR LESS
Paul begs mercy for a runaway slave converted to Christianity.

DETAILS, PLEASE
Philemon is a "fellowlabourer" (1:1) of Paul, a man who has "refreshed" (1:7) other Christians with his love and generosity. But the apostle writes with a deeper request—that Philemon forgive and take back a runaway slave, who apparently accepted Christ under Paul's teaching: "my son Onesimus, whom I have begotten in my bonds" (1:10). "If thou count me therefore a partner," Paul wrote to Philemon, "receive him as myself" (1:17).

QUOTABLE
I thank my God, making mention of thee always in my prayers, hearing of thy love and faith, which thou hast toward the Lord Jesus, and toward all saints. (1:4–5)

Having confidence in thy obedience I wrote unto thee, knowing that thou wilt also do more than I say. (1:21)

UNIQUE AND UNUSUAL
With only one chapter and twenty-five verses, Philemon is the shortest of Paul's letters in the Bible.

SO WHAT?
Christians are called to forgive, and here's a practical example to consider. With God's help, will you let go of your grudges?

HEBREWS

AUTHOR
Not stated; Paul, Luke, Barnabas, and Apollos have all been suggested.

DATE
Probably sometime before AD 70, since Hebrews refers to temple sacrifices. The Jerusalem temple was destroyed by Romans in AD 70.

IN TEN WORDS OR LESS
Jesus is better than any Old Testament person or sacrifice.

Details, Please

Written to Jewish Christians (hence the name "Hebrews"), this long letter emphasizes the superiority of Christianity to Old Testament Judaism. Jesus is "so much better" (1:4) than angels, Moses, and the previous animal sacrifices. "For if the blood of bulls and of goats, and the ashes of an heifer sprinkling the unclean, sanctifieth to the purifying of the flesh," Hebrews asks, "how much more shall the blood of Christ, who through the eternal Spirit offered himself without spot to God, purge your conscience from dead works to serve the living God?" (9:13–14). Jewish Christians, some of whom were apparently wavering in their commitment to Jesus, are reminded that Christ "is the mediator of a better covenant, which was established upon better promises" (8:6)—a once-for-all sacrifice on the cross that provides "eternal redemption for us" (9:12).

Quotable

How shal we escape, if we neglect so great salvation. (2:3)

There remaineth therefore a rest to the people of God. (4:9)
It is appointed unto men once to die, but after this the judgment. (9:27)

Not forsaking the assembling of ourselves together, as the manner of some is; but exhorting one another: and so much the more, as ye see the day approaching. (10:25)

Now faith is the substance of things hoped for, the evidence of things not seen. (11:1)

Wherefore seeing we also are compassed about with so great a cloud of witnesses, let us lay aside every weight, and the sin which doth so easily beset us, and let us run with patience the race that is set before us, looking unto Jesus the author and finisher of our faith. (12:1–2)

Let brotherly love continue. (13:1)

Unique and Unusual

Hebrews is one of only two New Testament letters (the other being 1 John) that includes no greeting or hint of its author.

So What?

"Having therefore, brethren, boldness to enter into the holiest by the blood of Jesus. . .let us draw near with a true heart in full assurance of faith, having our hearts sprinkled from an evil conscience, and our bodies washed with pure water" (10:19, 22).

JAMES

AUTHOR
James (1:1), probably a brother of Jesus (see Matthew 13:55; Mark 6:3).

DATE
Approximately AD 60.

IN TEN WORDS OR LESS
Real Christian faith is shown by one's good works.

DETAILS, PLEASE
Though the apostle Paul clearly taught that salvation is by faith alone and not by good works (see Romans 3:28), James clarifies that good works will *follow* true faith: "What doth it profit, my brethren, though a man say he hath faith, and have not works?" (2:14). James encourages Christians, in everyday life, to view trials as opportunities for spiritual growth, to control their tongues, to make peace, to avoid favoritism, and to help the needy. The bottom line? "Therefore to him that knoweth to do good, and doeth it not, to him it is sin" (4:17).

QUOTABLE
Draw nigh to God, and he will draw nigh to you. (4:8)

The effectual fervent prayer of a righteous man availeth much. (5:16)

UNIQUE AND UNUSUAL
For those who think it's enough just to believe in God, James says, "The devils also believe, and tremble" (2:19). Life-changing faith in Jesus is the key.

SO WHAT?
Want practical wisdom for living the Christian life? You'll find it all through the book of James.

1 PETER

AUTHOR
The apostle Peter (1:1), with the assistance of Silvanus (Silas, 5:12).

DATE
Approximately AD 65.

IN TEN WORDS OR LESS
Suffering for the sake of Jesus is noble and good.

DETAILS, PLEASE
As the early church grows, the Roman Empire begins persecuting Christians—

and Peter assures them that God is still in control: "Beloved, think it not strange concerning the fiery trial which is to try you, as though some strange thing happened unto you" (4:12). What is the proper response to such suffering? "Rejoice, inasmuch as ye are partakers of Christ's sufferings; that, when his glory shall be revealed, ye may be glad also with exceeding joy" (4:13).

QUOTABLE
Be sober, be vigilant; because your adversary the devil, as a roaring lion, walketh about, seeking whom he may devour. (5:8)

UNIQUE AND UNUSUAL
Peter clarifies exactly how many people rode out the great flood on Noah's ark: eight (3:20). Genesis indicates that "Noah. . .and his sons, and his wife, and his sons' wives" (Genesis 7:7) were in the boat but leaves unsaid whether any sons might have had multiple wives.

SO WHAT?
Life may be hard, but God is always good. And for Christians, there's a much better day ahead.

2 PETER

AUTHOR
The apostle Peter (1:1).

DATE
Probably the late 60s AD, shortly before Peter's execution.

IN TEN WORDS OR LESS
Beware of false teachers within the church.

DETAILS, PLEASE
The Christian qualities of faith, virtue, knowledge, self-control, patience, godliness, and love (1:5–8), coupled with a reliance on scripture (1:19–21), will help believers avoid the false teachings of those who "privily shall bring in damnable heresies, even denying the Lord that bought them" (2:1).

QUOTABLE
We have not followed cunningly devised fables, when we made known unto you the power and coming of our Lord Jesus Christ, but were eyewitnesses of his majesty. (1:16)

The Lord is not slack concerning his promise, as some men count slackness; but is longsuffering to us-ward, not willing that any should perish, but that all should come to repentance. (3:9)

Unique and Unusual

Peter wrote this letter knowing his death was near: "Shortly I must put off this my tabernacle, even as our Lord Jesus Christ hath shewed me" (1:14).

So What?

"Beware lest ye also, being led away with the error of the wicked, fall from your own stedfastness" (3:17).

1 John

Author

Not stated but according to church tradition, the apostle John.

Date

Approximately AD 92.

In Ten Words or Less

Jesus was real man just as He is real God.

Details, Please

First John tackles a strange heresy that claimed Jesus had been on earth only in spirit, not in body: "Every spirit that confesseth not that Jesus Christ is come in the flesh is not of God: and this is that spirit of antichrist" (4:3). John wrote that he knew Jesus personally, as one "which we have looked upon, and our hands have handled" (1:1), and that knowledge leads to a saving belief in Jesus. Saving belief leads to obedience, but even when we sin, we know that God "is faithful and just to forgive us our sins" when we confess (1:9).

Quotable

Beloved, let us love one another: for love is of God. . . . God is love. (4:7–8)

Unique and Unusual

First John includes none of the usual features of a Bible letter—greetings, identification of the author, and the like. But it's a very warm, compassionate letter nonetheless.

So What?

"These things have I written. . .*that ye may know that ye have eternal life*" (5:13, emphasis added).

2 John

Author

The apostle John according to church tradition. The author is identified only as "the elder" (1:1).

DATE
Approximately AD 92.

IN TEN WORDS OR LESS
Beware false teachers who deny Jesus' physical life on earth.

DETAILS, PLEASE
Addressed to "the elect lady and her children" (1:1), perhaps an actual family or, figuratively, a church, 2 John tackles the heretical idea that Jesus had not been physically present on earth. The letter may be a reaction to the "gnostics," who taught that Jesus was spirit only and that He just appeared to suffer and die on the cross. This teaching, of "a deceiver and an antichrist" (1:7), should be avoided at all costs—to the point of barring one's door against those who believe it (1:10).

QUOTABLE
I beseech thee, lady, not as though I wrote a new commandment unto thee, but that which we had from the beginning, that we love one another. (1:5)

This is love, that we walk after his commandments. (1:6)

UNIQUE AND UNUSUAL
Second John, one of the New Testament's four single-chapter books, is the shortest by verse count: thirteen.

SO WHAT?
Just as in John's time, false teachers spread dangerous ideas in today's world. Every teaching should be weighed against scripture, 2 John says. "He that abideth in the doctrine of Christ, he hath both the Father and the Son" (1:9).

3 JOHN

AUTHOR
The apostle John according to church tradition. The author is identified only as "the elder" (1:1).

DATE
Approximately AD 92.

IN TEN WORDS OR LESS
Church leaders must be humble, not proud.

DETAILS, PLEASE
Addressed to a believer named Gaius, 3 John praises those (like Gaius and another Christian named Demetrius) who lead in "charity before the church" (1:6). But 3 John also has harsh words for Christians like Diotrophes, "who loveth to have the preeminence" (1:9) and refuse to show kindness and hospitality to traveling evangelists.

QUOTABLE
I have no greater joy than to hear that my children walk in truth. (1:4)

He that doeth good is of God: but he that doeth evil hath not seen God. (1:11)

UNIQUE AND UNUSUAL
Third John, one of four single-chapter books in the New Testament, is the second shortest by verse count: fourteen.

SO WHAT?
Hospitality isn't just for the Martha Stewarts of the world—Christians are expected to feed, house, and encourage other believers, especially those who minister full-time for God. Humble service to others follows the example of Jesus Himself (see John 13:14).

JUDE

AUTHOR
Jude (1:1), possibly Jesus' half brother (see Matthew 13:55; Mark 6:3).

DATE
Approximately AD 82.

IN TEN WORDS OR LESS
Beware of heretical teachers and their dangerous doctrines.

DETAILS, PLEASE
Jude tackles the same problems Peter did in his second letter: false teachers who were leading the early church astray. "Murmurers" and "complainers" who were "walking after their own lusts" (1:16) were apparently using the grace of God as a cover for their sinful lifestyles—and encouraging Christian believers to do the same. True believers, Jude says, reflect God's love, show compassion, and work to pull sinners "out of the fire" (1:23).

QUOTABLE
Ye should earnestly contend for the faith which was once delivered unto the saints. (1:3)

UNIQUE AND UNUSUAL
Jude provides details of two Old Testament events not recorded in the Old Testament: the archangel Michael's fight with Satan over the body of Moses (1:9) and Enoch's prophecy of God's judgment (1:14–15).

SO WHAT?
Satan tries to sneak "secret agents" into God's church to confuse and ultimately crush true believers. It's the job of every true Christian to "earnestly contend for the faith" as passed down by Jesus' disciples and recorded in the Bible.

REVELATION

AUTHOR
John (1:1), probably the apostle.

DATE
Approximately AD 95.

IN TEN WORDS OR LESS
God will judge evil and reward His saints.

DETAILS, PLEASE
Jesus Christ Himself arranges for John to receive a "revelation" of "things which must shortly come to pass" (1:1). First, in chapters 2–3, Jesus gives John words of challenge and/or encouragement for seven churches—the good, the bad, and the in-between. Then the vision turns to the actual throne room of God, where a Lamb, looking "as it had been slain" (5:6), breaks seven seals from a scroll, unleashing war, famine, and other disasters on the earth. A dragon and two beasts, allied against God, arise to demand the worship of earth's people who have not been killed in the earlier catastrophes. The satanic forces and the people who follow them incur seven "vials of the wrath of God" (16:1), which bring plagues, darkness, and huge hailstones on earth. The upheaval destroys "Babylon the great," the evil and arrogant world system, just before an angel from heaven seizes Satan, "that old serpent" (20:2), and imprisons him for one thousand years. After a brief release to instigate a worldwide war, Satan is thrown into "the lake of fire and brimstone," where he will be "tormented day and night for ever and ever" (20:10). God unveils "a new heaven and a new earth" (21:1), where He will "wipe away all tears" (21:4) from His people's eyes.

QUOTABLE
Blessed is he that readeth, and they that hear the words of this prophecy, and keep those things which are written therein. (1:3)

Worthy is the Lamb that was slain to receive power, and riches, and wisdom, and strength, and honour, and glory, and blessing. (5:12)

UNIQUE AND UNUSUAL
Revelation is an example of "apocalyptic literature," the only such book in the New Testament. *Apocalyptic* implies "revealing secret information." The book of Revelation identifies Jesus Christ as the "Alpha and Omega" (1:8) and reveals the number 666 as a sign of "the beast" (13:18).

SO WHAT?
"I've read the back of the book," an old Southern gospel song says, "and we win!" God has given His children a preview of how this world ends—and the new-and-improved world we'll enjoy forever. The curse of sin will be gone, we'll live in perfect fellowship with the Lord Himself, and we will "reign for ever and ever" (22:5). Kind of puts our bad days in perspective, doesn't it?

How to Study the Bible

Robert M. West

To the men of God I've known throughout my life
who have taught me how to study the Bible.

Contents

Introduction

When you study the Bible, you'll discover what millions of people have found throughout the centuries: You're reading the Word of the living God. In times past, He spoke to His special servants audibly, in visions, in dreams; now His main method of revelation to all humanity is His written Word.

Over a period of fifteen hundred years, the Holy Spirit directed forty holy men of God, living on three continents, to write His words into sixty-six books. These writings were preserved and collected into the single volume we know as the Bible.

Though people wrote it, the Bible itself says God was its ultimate source. In 2 Timothy 3:16 (KJV), we read, "All scripture is given by inspiration of God," which literally means it was breathed out by God.

The New Testament gives several descriptive titles to the Bible: the Word of God, the oracles of God, the Word of Christ, the holy scriptures, the word of truth, and the word of life. In studying the Bible, we're learning God's Word, holy and true, which contains the knowledge of eternal life.

The people of Thessalonica (who received two letters from the apostle Paul, which became part of the Bible) recognized that the apostle was giving them the Word of God in his preaching and from his pen. First Thessalonians 2:13 (NASB) tells us, "For this reason we also constantly thank God that when you received the word of God which you heard from us, you accepted it not as the word of men, but for what it really is, the word of God."

Years ago, when I was a high school student, my reading skills were poor. I had difficulty understanding and retaining what I read. Later, when I realized that God communicates to us through His written Word, I concluded that if I wanted to know Him and His truth, I must give myself to studying His Word. I've studied the Bible for many years now, encouraged along the way by devoted Christians who love the Bible.

Many Christians have made this same decision, and virtually all will testify to the great spiritual blessings that come from studying God's Word. Having studied and taught the Bible now for more than thirty years, I'll share things I've learned through my own experience as well as what others have taught me.

My hope and prayer is that through reading this book, you'll be encouraged to become one of those believers who is taught by God, learning His Word and receiving the special blessings He's reserved for you.

If you're new to the Christian faith, you'll find helpful recommendations in this book. If you've been a Christian for a while but have struggled in your personal Bible study, you'll be encouraged and challenged to have victory in this area of your life. If you're reading this book as a mature believer established in Bible study, my intention is to stir you up—to remember those things you have already learned and to help others learn how to study God's truth. People in your life need to learn what God has taught you, and you can become an answer to their prayers for a person to help them.

Some may rationalize their lack of Bible study by saying that life is too busy or studying the Bible is too hard. Others, who struggle with sin, as I did early in my Christian life, may honestly admit that it's just too convicting to read. Please don't let excuses stop you from studying God's Word.

Jesus made it clear that learning and living the Bible is God's will for our lives. He said, "Man shall not live by bread alone, but by every word that proceeds from the mouth of God" (Matthew 4:4). Bible study isn't just a nice thing to do—it's essential to our lives!

1. PREPARATION

Readying Our Hearts for Bible Study

For the word of God is living and active and sharper than any two-edged sword, and piercing as far as the division of soul and spirit, of both joints and marrow, and able to judge the thoughts and intentions of the heart.

HEBREWS 4:12 NASB

People who want to learn how to study the Bible often ask, "Where do I begin?"

It's a good question, but the answer might be surprising. We actually begin with ourselves. We prepare our hearts to study the Bible.

Many activities in life require preparation. If we're going to exercise, we first stretch our muscles to avoid injuries. If we're going to do a job around the house, we first gather the tools and materials the job requires. If we're going on a trip, we first make sure our car is properly maintained, that we've packed everything we need, and that we have a good map.

We might be tempted to think we can just jump in without any kind of preparation, but we've all experienced what happens when we fail to prepare: problems and disappointments.

Studying the Bible also requires some preparation, so we can have a profitable time studying and avoid problems that might discourage us, leading us to give up. I'm talking about personal preparation that focuses on our hearts. This is something we can easily overlook, and if not addressed, contributes to the breakdown of daily Bible study.

Frequently the Bible uses the word *heart* in a figurative sense, referring to the innermost portions of our being—our thoughts, emotions, and will—rather than the physical heart. It's our hearts that interest the Lord. When the prophet Samuel was preparing to anoint the future king of Israel, the Lord told him, "Man looks at the outward appearance, but the LORD looks at the heart" (1 Samuel 16:7).

As we think about personal Bible study, we shouldn't view it as another intellectual exercise like the study of math, science, history, or anything else that interests us. When studying these disciplines, the mind is engaged, but not the heart. God wants us to increase our knowledge of His Word with our minds, but He also intends for the power of His Word to affect our hearts and that our lives will be changed to become more like Christ's.

Concern for a change of life was expressed by the Lord Jesus for His disciples when He prayed, "Sanctify them by Your truth. Your word is truth" (John 17:17).

Two disciples, who didn't recognize the resurrected Lord Jesus as He walked with them on the Emmaus Road, illustrate the experience of having the heart involved in learning God's Word. As they walked with Jesus, He began to teach them things about Himself from all of the Old Testament scriptures. Later that evening, as they recalled their experience, they said to each other, "Did not our heart burn within us while He talked with us on the road, and while He opened the Scriptures to us?" (Luke 24:32).

The hearts of these two disciples had previously been confused and discouraged as they thought the crucifixion of Jesus meant His defeat and end. When they finally recognized Him and He vanished from their presence, they considered how their hearts were warmed with spiritual revival and excitement. The spiritual heartburn they experienced was a good thing!

When our minds and our hearts are prepared and involved in Bible study, our time spent in God's Word is enjoyable and exciting.

People can have a good study Bible, have a few helpful study books, follow numerous recommended procedures, and have a quiet place to concentrate, and still not benefit spiritually from the time spent in the Bible because their hearts aren't prepared to be involved in the process. Their focus may be on only intellectual growth, not spiritual growth.

The religious leaders in Jesus' day, the scribes and Pharisees, made this error. They had a serious heart condition known as hypocrisy. Jesus described them this way: "These people draw near to Me with their mouth, and honor Me with their lips, but their heart is far from Me" (Matthew 15:8).

They were the kind of people who go through the motions of religious activity, more concerned about their artificial, external religious rules than about having their hearts right before God through faith and obedience to His Word. The human "heart," described as "deceitful above all things, and desperately wicked" in Jeremiah 17:9, is of major concern to God.

This chapter opened with the words of Hebrews 4:12. The context of this verse reveals that God knows everything about every one of us. As we read His Word, it functions as an X-ray machine or heart monitor, revealing to us what He sees in our hearts. Let's see ourselves as God sees us. His Word exposes our hearts so we can take corrective action (Hebrews 4:13).

Addressing issues of the heart was something that most of the scribes and Pharisees neglected to do, but Ezra, an Old Testament priest, "prepared his heart to seek the Law of the LORD" (Ezra 7:10). That's what we need to do as we begin Bible study.

I suggest that preparing our hearts means two things. First, we need to approach God's Word *dependently*. Second, we need to approach God's Word *purposefully*.

DEPENDENTLY

Depend on the Holy Spirit

Many people who begin to study the Bible will soon be saying, "I need help!" That's a good conclusion to come to. We all need help, and the person to help us is God. He gave us His Word and also assists us in understanding it. The technical term for this help is *illumination*. Let's look at a few New Testament verses describing God's work illuminating people's hearts.

On one occasion Jesus was teaching people about His Father's work in the lives of those who would be saved. He quoted the Old Testament when He said, "It is written in the prophets, 'And they shall all be taught by God' " (John 6:45). People who have come to know the Lord have experienced the illuminating work of God in their minds and hearts to understand their own lost, sinful condition and to see that Christ is the solution to their problem.

Paul spoke about illumination when he said, "But the natural man does not receive the things of the Spirit of God, for they are foolishness to him; nor can he know them, because they are spiritually discerned" (1 Corinthians 2:14).

The natural man refers to someone who hasn't been saved and therefore doesn't have the indwelling Holy Spirit. People in this condition reject the gospel message and view it as foolishness. Subjects such as sin, guilt, forgiveness, grace, and salvation don't make sense to them and don't have personal value. They don't have interest, understanding, trust, or appreciation for Christ and His Word because they haven't had the work of God's Spirit in their hearts. Christ's Word must be understood on a spiritual level, not just an intellectual level.

Even the apostles needed divine help for understanding. Before the risen Lord Jesus returned to heaven, He assisted them in understanding the Old Testament. "And He opened their understanding, that they might comprehend the Scriptures" (Luke 24:45). Even though these men learned the scriptures throughout their lives, they failed to understand all that the Word of God predicted about Jesus. They needed His help to finally see.

John Newton, the author of the beloved hymn "Amazing Grace," wrote in the lyrics of that song, "I once was lost but now am found, was blind but now I see." He was referring to his own experience of not grasping biblical truth as a person who was spiritually lost. When he was saved by God's grace, his spiritual blindness was healed so he could say, "Now I see."

The only person who can make the blind see is God, so He's the One we depend on to give us understanding of His Word. The first thing a person needs, simply put, is to be saved, to be totally dependent on God for all his or her spiritual needs. (See Acts 16:30–31.)

Once we have recognized our need for help from God to understand His Word, we should regularly pray for His assistance. The psalmist realized this and expressed dependence to God: "Open my eyes, that I may see wondrous things from Your law" (Psalm 119:18). This is a great prayer for us as well when we prepare our hearts to study His Word.

Depend on Mature Believers

Not only should we depend on the teaching ministry of the Holy Spirit, but we should also depend on mature believers who have a strong knowledge of God's Word.

According to the apostle Paul, God gives certain people a supernatural ability to teach the Word: "Having then gifts differing according to the grace that is given to us, let us use them. . .he who teaches, in teaching"(Romans

12:6–7). But teaching occurs in many settings, as Moses told the ancient Israelites: "These words, which I am commanding you today, shall be on your heart. You shall teach them diligently to your sons and shall talk of them when you sit in your house and when you walk by the way and when you lie down and when you rise up" (Deuteronomy 6:6–7 NASB). The design of God is that mature Christians teach His Word to others.

Just before He ascended into heaven, Jesus gave His apostles their final instructions, telling them, "Go therefore and make disciples of all the nations, baptizing them in the name of the Father and the Son and the Holy Spirit, *teaching them to observe all that I commanded you*" (Matthew 28:19–20 NASB, emphasis added). What Jesus commanded is recorded for us in the Bible—and the Holy Spirit and gifted teachers help us to understand and apply those commands to our own lives.

PURPOSEFULLY

By saying we must study the Bible purposefully, I mean we should be clear in our minds why we are spending part of our day studying. This is another part of personal preparation. We'd know why we were studying if we were to give a devotional message or share our thoughts about a biblical topic with a group. We'd be motivated by the specific task before us.

But what we're considering at this point are the reasons we're to be consistent in our everyday study habits. What is it that motivates us to study like the Berean Christians in Acts 17:11, who "searched the Scriptures daily"?

The best answers come straight from the Bible. The following sections describe what God would have us keep in mind so we'll be motivated to be faithful in our study. Call these the Top Ten Reasons for Personal Bible Study.

1. To settle the issue of our own salvation

Paul reminded Timothy about Timothy's own experience: "From child-hood you have known the Holy Scriptures, which are able to make you wise for salvation through faith which is in Christ Jesus" (2 Timothy 3:15). This is the primary issue that needs to be settled in everyone's life.

God uses His Word as a means to save sinners. As we think about our conversion, we may be able to identify Bible verses that God used in our lives to save us—or at least a believer's life-giving words that were based on scripture. God also wants us to have what the hymn writer Fanny Crosby called "blessed assurance." Many Christians experience doubts about their own conversion, and through learning those portions of scripture that address this subject, we can have a deepening confidence about our own salvation.

When people want to start reading the Bible, a good place to begin is the Gospel of John in the New Testament, because this book was specifically written so people might read about Christ, believe in Him, and receive the gift of eternal life from Him. (See John 20:30–31.) This book of the Bible was written with the purpose of helping those who read it find salvation in Christ.

2. To grow spiritually

New Christians are sometimes described as babes in Christ, and of course, all babies need to grow. Peter gave this instruction to Christians in the early church: "But grow in the grace and knowledge of our Lord and Savior Jesus Christ" (2 Peter 3:18).

He also gave a direct exhortation that they should have the same kind of desire for the basic truths of God's Word that a newborn baby has for milk. "As newborn babes, desire the pure milk of the word, that you may grow thereby" (1 Peter 2:2). This is a picture representing intense hunger for God's Word so that we can grow in our understanding and spiritual strength. The Bible repeatedly refers to itself as food for the soul. Just as our bodies need food to survive, our souls need the spiritual food of the Bible.

In Ephesians 4, Paul expressed the same concern as Peter for the growth of believers. He didn't want them to be tossed about and carried away with every wind of doctrine; he wanted them to be steady and strong. When we neglect to develop our understanding of truth, we can be more easily influenced by the error of false teachers. Spiritual growth through studying the Bible protects us from bad spiritual influence.

3. To receive personal blessing and encouragement

Paul wrote, "For whatever things were written before were written for our learning, that we through the patience and comfort of the Scriptures might have hope" (Romans 15:4). As believers, we often experience discouragement in our Christian walk. A common cause of this discouragement is conflict between believers, which Paul addresses in Romans 15. Difficulties between Christians, which create a lack of unity, can be discouraging. As we all eventually learn, there's no lack of tension and trouble in local churches. But as we study the Bible, we see Christ's example. How He interacted with people is the pattern we're to follow for living and for treating others.

When we study the Bible, we'll also read numerous promises God made to give believers hope, and stories about how God providentially worked in the lives of people. Meditating on all these passages of scripture encourages us to persevere in our own Christian life with comfort and hope.

Discouragement can also come from conviction about our sins as we're brought face-to-face with God's holy standards in the Bible. When we're honest about our lives, we have to admit we fall short of His glory. It's frustrating to struggle with the same sins over and over, not being able to break bad habits in our lives. But as we continue to read God's Word, we'll also discover the comfort and hope available to us through God's mercy, grace, and forgiveness in Christ.

We can learn about His power to transform our lives by the power of His Word. Reading about how He pardoned and delivered others—and then us—gives us hope. The God of patience and comfort wants us to be encouraged. Since the Bible was written for our education, the more we learn, the more we can be encouraged.

4. To receive personal guidance

When faced with many of life's decisions, we often wonder, *What should I do now?* Learning the Bible can be helpful in answering this question. "Your word is a lamp to my feet and a light to my path" (Psalm 119:105).

The psalmist pictured the effect of learning God's Word as having a lamp for life that lights the way before us so we can see where we're going.

As the nation of Israel journeyed in the wilderness after their exodus from Egypt, they were led by a pillar of fire at night. That was how God worked for that group of people at that time. What God has provided for us in our journey is His written Word, which gives us the light of knowledge and wisdom.

Many times the Bible addresses our specific situation, but when it doesn't, there are principles we can apply to our lives so we have confidence that we're being led by God's Word.

In Psalm 119, the psalmist refers to his daily experience of living in a world filled with spiritual and moral darkness, a world that calls good evil and evil good. As believers concerned with pleasing God and wanting to do His will, we try to make decisions that honor Him, but the influence of a dark world often makes this difficult. Through studying the Bible we learn what the will of God is and experience His direction.

As we seek God's guidance, he'll lead us by His Spirit (Romans 8:14), which always agrees with what God has revealed to us in His Word. His Spirit's leading never contradicts what He's written. If our personal decisions contradict what has been written in the Bible, then we can be sure we aren't being led by God.

5. To defend ourselves against the devil

Soon after we become Christians, we find out that the Christian life involves spiritual warfare. In Ephesians 6, Paul instructs believers with these words, "Put on the whole armor of God, that you may be able to stand against the wiles of the devil" (verse 11). The wiles of the devil are the methods he uses against people, trying to keep them from doing the will of God.

The Christian's defense against this assault is putting on the spiritual armor of God: Christian character and lifestyle empowered by God's Spirit. A vital part of this armor is "the sword of the Spirit, which is the word of God" (verse 17).

When the devil confronted Jesus in Matthew 4:1–10, tempting Him to act independently of God's will and questioning God's provision, protection, and plan, Jesus used God's Word to defend Himself. Three times in this story when the devil tempted him, Jesus responded, "It is written," and then quoted specific verses from Deuteronomy to rebuff the temptations. Jesus was able to draw from His knowledge of the Old Testament to overcome temptation by His knowledge of, trust in, and obedience to the Word.

In the apostle John's first letter, he refers to a group of young men, saying, "You are strong, and the word of God abides in you, and you have overcome the wicked one" (1 John 2:14). These believers withstood the devil's assault through their knowledge and application of scripture.

Through Bible study, we'll also be able to remember specific Bible verses, and by applying them, we'll be able to overcome the devil's temptations.

6. To effectively teach God's truth to the next generation

Deuteronomy 6:4–9 is known to Jews as the *Shema* (Hebrew for *hear*, the first word of the passage), and devout Jews recite it twice daily. It gives instruction about loving God, His Word, and loving our children by teaching them God's Word. "And these words which I command you today shall be in your heart. You shall teach them diligently to your children, and shall talk of them when you sit in your house, when you walk by the way, when you lie down, and when you rise up" (Deuteronomy 6:6–7). Parents teaching their children is God's pattern for the Christian home.

Parents aren't simply to teach their children, but to teach them diligently. The text also reveals that the teaching is informal, given throughout the day, inside and outside the home. Parents are the primary teachers of their children, and they can only do this effectively if they first learn God's Word themselves.

Parents are to have answers for their children when questioned about God's Word. Moses confirmed this when he wrote, "When your son asks you in time to come, saying, 'What is the meaning of the testimonies, the statutes, and the judgments which the LORD our God has commanded you?' then you shall say to your son. . ." (Deuteronomy 6:20–21). Parents have only a limited amount of time to teach their children before the children are grown and begin their own lives. I can testify that the time, although it's years long, goes by quickly. So studying the Bible ourselves helps us in this important task.

7. To be able to counsel others

God wants to use us to provide knowledge about what He has said in His Word to others. "Let the word of Christ dwell in you richly in all wisdom, teaching and admonishing one another" (Colossians 3:16). In time, God wants to use you to help others who may be newer to the faith. We might be able to remember with gratitude and fondness older Christians who helped us when we wondered what the Bible said about a particular subject.

We should notice what Colossians 3:16 says about learning the Bible: The word of Christ is "to dwell in you." This literally means to be at home in you. The word of Christ is to take up residence in us, influencing every part of our lives. The text goes on to say that the word should "dwell in you richly in all wisdom," indicating that we're to have a full understanding of the Bible. Then we can be a good friend providing wise counsel.

8. To be ready to speak with unbelievers about Christ

"But sanctify the Lord God in your hearts: and be ready always to give an answer to every man that asketh you a reason of the hope that is in you" (1 Peter 3:15 KJV). The concern of Christians shouldn't be winning arguments but winning people. We should be able to answer questions when we're asked and to give an explanation about our faith. Some people who won't listen to a sermon may want to find out about Christ in a private conversation, and we're told to be ready. The more we learn through studying, the more effective we'll become in sharing God's truth with others.

9. To verify that the teaching of others is the truth of God

One group of early Christians, the Bereans, stood out from the rest. "They received the word with all readiness, and searched the Scriptures daily to find out whether these things were so" (Acts 17:11). They checked in scripture to confirm what Paul taught them was true. They were so committed to this that they did it daily. It's a mistake for us to accept the message of Christian teachers just because they're humorous, dynamic, on television or radio, or have written books. The content of their message must be true, and it's good for us to validate it from our own study. Bible teachers should never be offended that people do this; they should encourage it.

10. To present ourselves approved to God

"Be diligent to present yourself approved to God as a workman who does not need to be ashamed, accurately handling the word of truth" (2 Timothy 2:15 NASB). Learning God's truth involves the work of studying.

Like divers who work to locate pearls in the ocean or miners who labor to find gold in the earth, Christians are workers who study the Bible to discover God's truth. We live our lives before God, and as servants we're to regularly present our lives to Him to be examined. We hope to have a sense of His approval and eventually hear from Him, "Well done, good and faithful servant." Divine approval comes from diligently studying God's Word so we can accurately share it with others.

When we approach God's Word in dependence on Him and more mature believers, we're progressing toward successful Bible study. When we approach His Word with the purpose of knowing God and His ways better, we're also making strides toward successful study. God's Word is truly "living and active," ready to change us from the inside out.

2. INTERPRETATION
Discovering What the Bible Means

Be diligent to present yourself approved to God as a workman who does not need to be ashamed, accurately handling the word of truth.
2 TIMOTHY 2:15 NASB

I vividly remember my high school history teacher responding to a student who had just misquoted the Bible in an attempt to prove a point in a classroom discussion. The teacher said, "You can make the Bible mean anything you want it to mean." Even at that young age, I was left with the impression that the Bible should be understood carefully, not carelessly.

Frequently people discussing the meaning of the Bible say, "Oh, that's just your interpretation." Is there a way to figure out what it means? The answer is a resounding yes! In this chapter, I'll share a number of guidelines to help you interpret the Bible properly.

Whether we realize it or not, we all interpret the Bible whenever we try to understand its meaning and make applications to our lives. The fact that we're already doing this shows how important it is that we learn to interpret correctly.

ONE INTERPRETATION, MANY APPLICATIONS

A good thought to begin with is this: Each verse of scripture has only one intended meaning even though there may be many applications. The Bible isn't written to mean different things to different people. The issue in every verse is always what God means by it, not what it means to me.

When interpreting a biblical text, there are a number of things to consider. Some texts clearly apply to everyone everywhere, while other texts apply only to people in the Bible who lived in a former time. Some things are to be understood literally, and others figuratively.

Some people bring their personal circumstances to texts of scripture and may wrongly think that God is speaking directly to them in some mysterious and secret way from a particular text.

You may have heard the anecdote about the man who opened his Bible and pointed to a verse hoping God would give him a personal message where his finger landed. He happened to place his finger on Matthew 27:5 and read, "He. . .departed, and went and hanged himself."

Perplexed about what this meant for him, he tried again, turning to another section, and his finger landed on Luke 10:37: "Then Jesus said to him, 'Go and do likewise.' "

Starting to get nervous, he tried again. Turning to John 13, he placed his finger on verse 27, "Then Jesus said to him, 'What you do, do quickly.'"

This funny story illustrates some people's casual and mystical approach to understanding the Bible.

In a personal experience, one day I had a doctor's appointment to get test results on what had the potential to be a serious ailment. That morning, I spent time in prayer and reading my Bible, where I happened to be reading Jeremiah 46. When I came to verse 11, I read these words: "In vain you will use many medicines; you shall not be cured."

Now if I hadn't learned how to interpret the Bible, this would have been a troubling verse. But it wasn't a direct, mystical message from God to me. It was actually addressed to the "daughter of Egypt," and I was glad! Later that day I received good news from the doctor, which confirmed to me that properly interpreting the Bible can save us from unnecessary anxiety.

Poor interpretation comes from preconceived ideas, bad theology, being too hasty in reaching conclusions, and ignoring principles of interpretation. This is why it's so important to learn basic guidelines that help us learn what God means by what He said.

WORTH THE INVESTMENT

You may think you're getting into more work than you want to do, but I encourage you to overcome the temptation to think that it won't be worth it. Some of the best time we spend in our lives will be spent studying the Bible. This isn't just tedious academics, but examining a love letter, the message of a God who loves us. Realizing this makes the time we spend studying enjoyable.

The time and work you invest will be rewarded by great discoveries of precious truth. Miners who search for gold or other precious metals keep their minds fixed on the value of the discovery they hope to make. They know they must devote time to their task. If you hear about a microwave Bible study plan—that is, a plan that lets you get it done quickly—my advice is to ignore it, because it won't be that beneficial.

It's been said that the Bible wasn't written for scholars, but for sinners. It's a book for all of us. Many parts are more difficult than others, but this shouldn't discourage us. Even Peter said that some of the things written by his beloved brother Paul were hard to understand (2 Peter 3:15–16).

A wise pastor once told me as I was beginning to learn God's Word that Bible study is like lifting weights. We start out lifting light weights and eventually work our way up to heavy weights. As we read and study the Bible, we don't have to be overly concerned by those things we don't understand. To switch the metaphor, all we need to do is grab the cookies from the shelf we *can* reach. As we read God's Word daily, we will grow in understanding and be able to deal with more difficult doctrines later.

Watch Out for False Teachers

As a warning to those who want to understand God's Word, the Bible speaks of false teachers who manipulate what the Bible says and who can be a bad influence if we don't guard ourselves against them. Jesus criticized the Sadducees of His day, who denied physical resurrection. "You are mistaken, not knowing the Scriptures" (Matthew 22:29). These men explained away certain Old Testament texts and spiritualized others, resulting in serious error.

Paul spoke of some religious and educated people living in the last days when he said that they are "always learning and never able to come to the knowledge of the truth. . .these also resist the truth" (2 Timothy 3:7–8).

False teachers often redefine biblical words, so we must check to make sure we understand how they are using them or God's intended meaning of verses becomes lost.

Peter described how some people misuse God's Word with horrifying results. He said, "Untaught and unstable people twist [Paul's words] to their own destruction, as they do also the rest of the Scriptures" (2 Peter 3:16). These people play fast and loose with the scriptures, ignoring proper principles of interpretation.

Since we live in the day where there's a battle for the truth, it's important for Christians to be discerning about books, programs, and teachers. I'm glad for all Bible-believing Christians who've had great influence on the world through the media, but we should always be cautious, because it's difficult at times to tell who are wolves in sheep's clothing (Matthew 7:15).

Though there is agreement on the fundamentals of the faith by true believers, there are also in-house debates. Unfortunately, Christians who know the Lord and handle the Bible accurately still have disagreements about what certain passages of the Bible mean. This has resulted in division among Christian individuals and Christian denominations. Differences exist over the nature of the Bible, the age of the earth, divine election, eternal security, gifts of the Spirit, the ritual of baptism, and the timing of the rapture, just to name a few.

Differences between believers will exist until the Lord returns. At that time, He will answer all questions and unify all believers. Until that day comes, we must do our best to love the brethren we disagree with and learn how to interpret the Bible as well as we can.

INDUCTIVE BIBLE STUDY

In learning to interpret scripture, we must discuss inductive Bible study, which seeks to discover the facts and details in a text and to draw conclusions about the meaning of a text from those observations. Inductive study has a sequence of three components: observation, interpretation, and application.

- Observation answers the question, *What does it say?* What is the actual content in the text?
- Interpretation answers the question, *What does it mean?* Our task is to discover the original intent and meaning of the author.
- Application answers the questions, *What does it mean to me?* and *How does it apply to my life?*

When we use this sequence, we'll find information and ideas that might have been overlooked otherwise. When this type of study isn't practiced, the door to interpretive abuses opens.

Observation

Observation always comes first. Before we consider what a text means, we must ask what it says. This means reading and rereading a text until we become acquainted with it. Occasionally, after I've taught about some part of the Bible, people have asked me with surprise, "How do you get all of that out of one verse?" Part of the answer is learning to be observant.

Most of us have watched television shows where a crime scene is being investigated. The area is taped off, and the authorities begin looking for clues. As clues are found—a footprint or a piece of clothing, perhaps—the detective places a bright marker at the location. A trained eye takes in many clues. Pictures are taken of the scene to be studied later. Evidence is taken to the lab, where even more information is revealed. Many people are involved in a slow process to discover the truth about what happened. This is observation, discovering all that can be found.

As a kid, I grew up watching *Dragnet*, a police show. One of the main characters was Detective Joe Friday. One of his trademark statements was, "Just the facts, ma'am." He wasn't interested in opinions or feelings. All he wanted was factual evidence. During the observation stage, we're also looking for the facts.

In developing our observation skills, we'll find it helpful to ask a series of questions. We can use them for any text. Put your text under a light and interrogate it! We just want the facts. Texts will have answers for most of the following questions.

- *Who?* Who was writing? To whom was the message originally written? Who are the people involved in the scenario?
- *What?* What's happening? What's said? Is it a command, an exhortation, a rebuke, a question, an answer, a prayer, a quotation of other scripture, something else? What's the main point? What key words or phrases are used? What's the context? What literary style is being used? Is it narrative, conversation, parable, prophecy, poetry, a letter, or a sermon?
- *When?* Are there time references? Are there words related to the past, present, or future? Look for words like *after, until, then*.
- *Where?* Are there locations mentioned—towns, roads, rivers,

mountains, regions, or other landmarks?

- *Why?* Are there any clues about why things are being said or done?
- *How?* Is there an explanation about how things are done?

These six questions help us gain information to see what a text actually says.

Interpretation

The ultimate interpretation question is, *What did God mean by what He said?* Interpretation is determining the meaning of a text once all of the facts are in. Compiling evidence from our observation takes some time, and we must guard against jumping to premature conclusions. New evidence can influence our conclusions, so we shouldn't be too hasty in moving to this part of the inductive process. We can see a clear example of this in the judicial system where some verdicts have been overturned when advances in DNA testing provided new evidence.

Some of us have been in Bible study classes where the facilitator asked *What does this passage mean to you?* before the group observed the facts and determined what the author intended. This is a good question when asked at the right time because it forces people to think about the Bible, but it's not a good question to ask first because people speak offhandedly before they give thought to the text. In this situation, interpreting the Bible becomes totally subjective, meaning different things to different people.

But every verse in the Bible means only one thing—what the original author intended—and that's what we're trying to discover. Interpretation of the Bible isn't a matter of personal opinion, feelings, or democratic agreement; it's a matter of gathering evidence from the text and following established principles of interpretation. Some people innocently make the error of reading a text, skipping interpretation altogether, and jumping to application.

John MacArthur tells the story of one of his assistant pastors, who counseled a couple who married as a result of a sermon preached on the destruction of Jericho. The pastor at a previous church had taught that God's people claimed the city, marched around it seven times, and the walls fell down. Then he explained to the young men that if a man believed God had given him a particular single young girl, he could claim her, walk around her seven times, and the walls of her heart would fall down! Of all the lessons to be learned about the fall of Jericho, lessons about marriage aren't among them.

2 Timothy 2:15 (NASB) speaks of "accurately handling the word of truth." In Greek, *accurately handling* literally means "cutting a straight line." When Paul, a tent maker, wrote to Timothy, he may have had in mind cutting material in a straight line to sew pieces of a tent together. Paul and Timothy needed to be precise and accurate in interpreting and teaching the Bible so it would all fit together without contradiction. They were to cut straight or handle straight the word of truth. Shame waits for those workers who mishandle the word of truth.

When we're trying to discover the meaning of the text, many times it's plain; it's on the surface of what we read. Alistair Begg, of the radio program *Truth for Life*, speaks repeatedly about "the main things and the plain things" when studying the Bible. Focus first on what is clear and obvious.

David Cooper, founder of the Biblical Research Society, established the golden rule of interpretation. The short version is, "If the plain sense makes good sense, seek no other sense or it will result in nonsense." Apply his rule first and work from there. Don't sacrifice plain meaning for unique, mystical, or obscure ideas.

Once we have asked the six observation questions of the text, we then apply six principles of interpretation.

1. The literal principle

The literal principle means interpreting the Bible with the normal meaning of words while recognizing figures of speech like symbolism, allegory, and metaphor. God has communicated with us through written language, so we should understand the words of scripture the way we use them in everyday life. Let a text speak for itself. When Jesus was born, it was a literal virgin birth. The miracles He preformed were real. His death and resurrection were actual historical events.

We recognize that many portions of scripture, especially poetry and prophecy, are filled with figurative language. Psalm

91:4 is an example of figurative language in Hebrew poetry: "He shall cover you with His feathers, and under His wings you shall take refuge." This doesn't mean that God has feathers and wings; rather it provides an image of God as our protector the same way a bird protects its young by covering them with its wings.

A prophetic example comes from Revelation 1:16: "He had in His right hand seven stars, out of His mouth went a sharp two-edged sword." Literal interpretation doesn't suggest seven actual stars or a real sword. The symbolic meaning of the stars is explained in Revelation 1:20, while the meaning of the sword is found in Revelation 2:16 and 19:15.

When the literal principle is used, the Bible is much easier to understand. There's no need to uncover hidden meanings.

2. The historical principle

The Bible must be understood in its historical setting before it can be fully understood in our contemporary setting. Bible students now become historians. We want to discover the original intent of the author by asking, *What did he mean by what he wrote?* Would our interpretation make sense to the first recipients? Before we ask what a text means to us, we must first ask what it meant to the original audience.

It's helpful to investigate the lifestyle and customs of that day, such as foot washing (1 Timothy 5:9–10), praying on a housetop (Acts 10:9), and girding the loins (1 Peter 1:13). Learning about the political and social backgrounds sheds light on certain texts. The Bible study tools mentioned in chapter 4 will prove helpful when studying historical background.

3. The contextual principle

The contextual principle means we should interpret a verse by the verses that surround it. You may have noticed that some verses begin in the middle of a sentence, so it's best to at least go back to the beginning of the sentence to get the flow of the author's thought. Some Bible teachers have said that context is so important that a verse of scripture should never be read by itself; it should always be read in its context to get the author's intended meaning.

The reason for this stance is summarized in this adage: A text out of context becomes a pretext for a proof text! In simpler words, this means a Bible verse standing alone can be misunderstood or misused to prove an error.

When Satan tempted Jesus and suggested that He should throw Himself down from the top of the temple, the devil quoted Bible verses out of context, giving them a wrong meaning. A psalm about trusting God was twisted into meaning that it's all right to test God (Matthew 4:5–6 and Psalm 91:11–12.) Jesus corrected the devil's error by quoting another text that rectified the wrong idea (Matthew 4:7 and Deuteronomy 6:16).

It's best to get the big picture of a text, then the context, and finally the details. This is starting with the bird's-eye view and going down to the worm's-eye view.

- Find out the general theme of the book.
- Determine the emphasis of each chapter and how it relates to the book theme.
- Find the paragraph divisions and how they relate to the thrust of each chapter.
- Dig into the verses to get each one's main idea and how they relate to each other.
- Go deeper into verses by doing word studies.

This digging makes our conclusions much more accurate.

4. The compatibility principle

The basic premise of the compatibility principle is to compare verses or passages of scripture with other scripture to see how they fit together. The best commentary on the Bible is the Bible, so we let it interpret itself. Properly understood, the Bible doesn't contradict itself; it complements itself. If our interpretations contradict what the Bible says elsewhere, we need to change our conclusions. As we study a text or subject, other portions of scripture shed light on it for fuller understanding. For example, doctrinal truth is spread throughout the Bible.

I remember the first time I seriously read the Gospels, the first four books of the New Testament. I read Matthew, then Mark. By the time I had completed Luke, I knew I had read its stories before—and I had, in Matthew and Mark. I eventually learned that these books all present the life of the Lord Jesus, giving different details to provide a complete picture of His life. The four authors were like a quartet harmonizing. They were singing the same song but hitting different notes. Comparing scripture with scripture is a safeguard against error and contradiction.

5. The grammatical principle

It shouldn't surprise us to learn the grammatical principle has to do with grammar and sentence structure. Recognizing parts of speech and the way they relate to each other can reveal a lot about a biblical text.

Seven easily overlooked but important words are *therefore*, *and*, *but*, *that*, *for*, *because*, and *if*. Examples of these are found in Romans 11–12.

In Romans 12:1, Paul writes, "I beseech you *therefore*, brethren, by the mercies of God, that you present your bodies a living sacrifice" (emphasis added). When we see the word *therefore*, we need to find out what it's there for. Find out what thoughts have gone before. In the first eleven chapters of Romans, Paul has laid the great foundation of the mercies of God by describing in detail God's plan of salvation. Paul then draws his thoughts to a practical conclusion in 12:1 and begs the Romans to present themselves to God as dedicated servants. He connects his practical appeal to his lengthy description of God's plan by the word *therefore*.

Verse 2 continues: "*And* do not be conformed to this world, *but* be transformed by the renewing of your mind, *that* you may prove what is that good and acceptable and perfect will of God." *And* introduces an addition, *but* points to a contrast, and *that* is used to begin a conclusion. Paul adds another appeal after his first one in verse 1 by using the word *and* at the beginning of verse 2. Then he presents a contrast with the word *but*. Paul exhorts believers not to succumb to external pressure to live and think like the unbelieving world, *but* to be internally transformed by renewing their thought life. (By the way, the source for renewed thinking is the Bible. See Psalm 1:1–2).

That (along with *for* and *because*) is used to introduce a purpose or reason at the end of verse 2. The reason for having our thinking renewed and our life transformed is so we can have confidence that we know and are doing the will of God.

In verse 19, the word *for* is also used to introduce a reason: Paul has written that Christians shouldn't be vengeful *for* the scriptures say we shouldn't.

An example of the use of *because,* also meaning purpose or reason, is found in Romans 11:20: "*Because* of unbelief they were broken off."

If is used in Romans 12:18: "*If* it is possible, as much as depends on you, live peaceably with all men." This word is used when a condition is present. Paul's point here is that Christians are always to be peacemakers, and if there is a lack of peace between a Christan and another person, it should never be the Christian's fault.

Considering these seven words helps us better understand the structure and meaning of a text.

6. The Christological principle

Jesus Christ is the main theme of the entire Bible, so keeping an eye out for references to Him as we study is important. The ministry of the Holy Spirit is to point us to Christ. "But when the Helper comes. . . the Spirit of truth. . .will testify of Me" (John 15:26).

Jesus said to unbelieving Jews of His day, "You search the

Scriptures, for in them you think you have eternal life; and these are they which testify of Me. . . . For if you believed Moses, you would believe Me; for he wrote about Me" (John 5:39, 46). Moses wrote the first five books of the Old Testament, so we look for Christ there.

At the end of His earthly ministry, Jesus told His apostles, "All things must be fulfilled which were written in the Law of Moses and the Prophets and the Psalms concerning Me" (Luke 24:44). Therefore, we also look for Jesus in the prophetic books and the psalms.

One day, an Ethiopian eunuch was reading the Old Testament text of Isaiah, which contains a prophecy about the Lord Jesus. A believer, Philip, helped him understand what he was reading. "Then Philip opened his mouth, and beginning at this Scripture [Isaiah 53:7–8], preached Jesus to him" (Acts 8:35). We should always be looking for Christ.

Application

Now we come to application, the third component of inductive Bible study. This answers the question, *How does this passage apply to me?* Bible study doesn't end with interpretation; it continues to the question, *So what?* The goal of Bible study isn't only gaining information but also experiencing transformation. We're not just trying to get through the Bible; we're letting the Bible get through us. If there's a good example, follow it. If there's a warning, heed it. If there's a command, obey it. If there's a promise, believe it.

Jesus prayed for all believers just before he died: "Sanctify them by Your truth. Your word is truth" (John 17:17). This is Jesus' request to God the Father that He use His word to influence believers to live lives set apart for His purposes. Our lifestyle is to be affected by the Bible as well as our beliefs, and this requires a humble response of doing the will of God.

James said that what should characterize believers is being "doers of the word, and not hearers only" (James 1:22). Self-deception is talking ourselves out of obeying the Bible and therefore cheating ourselves out of the blessings of God that accompany obedience. Some people mark their

Bibles, but their Bible seldom marks them.

Jesus spoke of the blessing of obedience and the foolishness of self-deception when He ended the Sermon on the Mount. He described two types of people, the obedient and disobedient, as builders. The obedient are like the man who built his house on a rock, which was able to stand when the storm came. The disobedient are like the man who built on a foundation of sand and experienced the destruction of his house when the storm came (Matthew 7:24–27). These two people both heard the truth but responded differently. One only *learned* it, while the other truly *lived* it.

Paul states in 2 Timothy 3:16 that scripture is inspired by God and is beneficial for four things, three having a practical emphasis. "All Scripture is given by inspiration of God, and is profitable for doctrine, for reproof, for correction, for instruction in righteousness." Paul is saying scripture is valuable for information to believe, to use as the perfect standard of right and wrong, for being restored after we've sinned, and for remaining restored. These four benefits are to make believers complete so that they can do whatever God has called them to do (verse 17).

Interpreting the Bible then includes the six observation questions, the six interpretation principles, and the necessary application to our lives.

3. CLASSIFICATION

Examining Bible Study Methods

> *Now [the Bereans] were more noble-minded than those in Thessalonica, for they received the word with great eagerness, examining the Scriptures daily to see whether these things were so.*
>
> Acts 17:11 nasb

As the Berean believers studied the scriptures in an attempt to verify the truthfulness of Paul's preaching, they were thorough in their approach to

God's Word and more than likely using some of study methods that I'll suggest in this chapter. All methods of Bible study have value in learning God's Word, but whatever method we use, the point to remember is that *studying the Bible* is what's important. It's to our benefit to pursue the habit of daily reading and studying God's Word.

The usefulness of knowing a variety of Bible study methods is that it helps us be flexible in our approach to scripture as we concentrate on a particular text, subject, or even a word. It also contributes to balancing our learning.

BALANCE

Before looking at different methods of Bible study, some thoughts about being balanced in our study are appropriate.

Old Testament/New Testament

I highly recommend balance in Bible study by using a variety of methods. For example, time spent studying the New Testament should be balanced by study of the Old Testament. It's not surprising that believers living under the new covenant want to spend their time in the New Testament learning about Jesus Christ and His gospel, but the Old Testament is quoted in the New Testament about 250 times. It's been said, "The new is in the old contained, and the old is in the new explained."

When the Bereans were searching the scriptures, they were studying the Old Testament. The New Testament was in the process of being written at that time. Early Christians had a solid foundation of Old Testament truth, and New Testament truth was added as it gradually became available. This is what's meant by the idea that God's revelation has been progressive.

The amazing preacher Apollos is an example of a person receiving progressive revelation. His preaching from the Old Testament was powerful and accurate as far as it went, but his knowledge was limited. Aquila and Priscilla, believers who heard him teach, shared more of God's revelation with him, and Apollos grew to become more effective in serving Christ (Acts 18:24–28).

Doctrine/Christian Living

Another area is balancing the study of Bible doctrine with the study of practical Christian living and how to apply doctrinal truth to everyday life.

Paul's preaching did this. He said to the Ephesian elders, "I have not shunned to declare to you the whole counsel of God" (Acts 20:27). The "whole counsel of God" is an all-inclusive term related to God's revelation covering both doctrine and duty in the Christian life. There was no subject that he intentionally omitted from his teaching. His preaching was well rounded because, in part, he wanted his hearers to be the same.

This is how our study should be so we gain a wider spectrum of truth and a good foundation of understanding we can build on.

Some Christians seem content to only occasionally study those things that spark their interest, while others have a diet of the latest Christian books that hit the bestseller list. My intention isn't to be critical of popular Christian books, for all pursuit of truth is helpful, but I'm concerned about poor study habits that sometimes neglect using the Bible altogether.

The point needs to be made that we should be involved in a balanced Bible study plan that uses a variety of techniques. In physical health, eating only those foods that we might enjoy—like snacks and sweets—won't contribute to good health. A balanced diet is required. This is equally true when we study the Bible.

Six Important Bible Study Methods

1. The Expositional Method

Expositional Bible study means studying individual Bible books verse by verse, using the observation, interpretation, and application guidelines from chapter 2. The benefit of this method is that it reveals the flow of the author's thoughts throughout the book, which contributes to a more accurate understanding of individual verses. This method requires more thinking about how verses relate to each other but leads to greater understanding in the long run. Bible commentaries are especially helpful with this method.

2. The Survey Method

When we use the survey method, we study Bible books as a whole to become acquainted with general information rather than the details of each verse. We investigate subjects like the author, where he's writing from, his style of writing, the theme, important topics contained in the book, who it was written for, and issues or circumstances the recipients might have been facing. Looking at the political background and chronology of events may explain why certain events happened.

We can also survey the entire Old or New Testament so we understand how the books of the Bible are divided and relate to each other. The thirty-nine Old Testament books can be divided into five categories:

- Genesis through Deuteronomy, the first five books, are known as the Law or the *Pentateuch* (meaning five volumes).
- Joshua through Esther are the twelve historical books.
- Job through Song of Solomon are the five poetic books.
- Isaiah through Daniel are the five major prophets.
- Hosea through Malachi are the twelve minor prophets.

The Old Testament was originally written in Hebrew, with some small sections written in Aramaic. They deal primarily with God's relationship with His chosen nation, Israel.

The twenty-seven New Testament books, originally written in Greek, can be divided into four categories:

- The four Gospels and Acts are the historical books.
- Romans through Philemon, the next thirteen books, are letters of the apostle Paul to churches or individuals.
- Hebrews through Jude, the next eight books, are called the general letters.
- Revelation, a prophetic book, appropriately ends the New Testament.

Bible encyclopedias, Bible dictionaries, and Old and New Testament overviews are all helpful when surveying the Bible.

3. The Topical Method

Occasionally we have a specific topic from the Bible we're interested in studying. We want to accumulate all the Bible says about it and then organize the information. A Bible concordance and a topical Bible guide us to specific verses about topics throughout the Bible. Then we can see how each subject is addressed in the Old Testament and the New Testament, and by individual biblical authors.

This method was especially helpful to me as a young Christian because I had so many doctrinal questions. One of the first study books I read was *Major Bible Themes* by Lewis Sperry Chafer (later revised by John Walvoord), a book of fifty-two Bible doctrines. I concentrated on particular subjects to better learn what God had to say about them.

There's a vast list of doctrines and subjects in the Bible. A Bible encyclopedia provides extensive articles on many topics.

The weakness of topical Bible study is that verses can be misunderstood if taken out of context.

4. The Biographical Method

Individual people in the Bible are of interest, so we may want to develop a character sketch. The Bible mentions over twenty-nine hundred people, some by name only. As with a topical method of study, we can use a concordance to find every Bible verse where the name is found. We have to take care to be sure that the texts all refer to the same person. Six women in the Bible are named Mary, five men are named John, and five men are named James.

Through faith in God's power, believers have accomplished some amazing things. (See Hebrews 11.) These people are examples for us and are called *witnesses,* who testify how God can empower his children to do His will.

God doesn't hide the weaknesses of His servants. David, the man after God's own heart, sinned in the matter of Uriah the Hittite (1 Kings 15:5). The apostle Peter denied the Lord (Matthew 26:69–74). Elijah was a man just like us (James 5:17). This kind of information encourages us. Through their experiences, we learn that God is forgiving and patient and that He is the God of second chances.

When developing a character sketch, study books such as *All the Men of the Bible* and *All the Women of the Bible* (by Herbert Lockyer) or *Twelve Ordinary Men* and *Twelve Extraordinary Women* (by John MacArthur) may prove helpful.

5. The Word Study Method

When a person is new to the Christian faith, some terms may be unfamiliar. Words like *propitiation, redemption, imputation, justification,* and *sanctification* are basic to the message of God's salvation in scripture. The words of scripture are the words that God inspired, so they become part of our study. God wants us to understand them. By using a concordance, you'll be able to locate these words and see how they're used.

Several Greek words might be translated into one English word. Using a study tool like a *Strong's Exhaustive Concordance* is essential to understanding the variety of meanings. Let's consider a few examples.

The World

Three Greek words all translate into the English word *world.* The Greek word *kosmos* is used in John 3:16: "For God so loved the world that He gave His only begotten Son." This refers to the world order of unsaved people who are opposed to God and controlled by Satan.

The Greek word *aion* is used in Romans 12:2: "And do not be conformed to this world." It refers to the particular age in which we live that's influential with false ideas and evil. J. B. Phillips translates this, "Don't let the world around you squeeze you into its mold."

The Greek word *oikoumene* is used in Matthew 24:14: "And this gospel of the kingdom will be preached in all the world." Matthew is referring to the inhabited world of people.

Love

We use the English word *love* for three Greek words that have slightly different meanings. The conversation that the risen Lord Jesus had with Peter in John 21:15–19 uses two of the Greek words.

Since Peter denied knowing the Lord three times, Jesus asked Peter three times if he really loved Him. In the first two questions, Jesus uses the Greek word *agape*, which refers to self-sacrificing love (also used in John 3:16). In Peter's answer he uses another Greek word for word for love, *phileo*, which emphasizes only fondness, probably because he still feels too much shame to use the word emphasizing a total loving devotion.

When Jesus asks the same question for the third time, He questions even Peter's fondness for Him by also using the word that Peter did, *phileo*. This intentional change of Greek words by Jesus is missed in our English Bible, but it's the reason why Peter was grieved.

Day

Context also has an important bearing on the meaning of words. The word *day*, for example, as used in the Bible, has several meanings that are determined by the context. In Genesis 1:5 there are two meanings: The twelve hours of light are called *day*, and the twenty-four-hour period indicated by the repeated phrase, "the evening and the morning" is also called *day*. When the word *day* appears with a numerical adjective (first day, second day), it consistently refers to a twenty-four-hour period. In Genesis 2:4, *day* also refers to the entire creative week. In Psalm 20:1, *day* refers to an indefinite period of time.

6. The Devotional Method

Many Christians use the phrase "having personal devotions" when referring to the devotional method. This type of study is less technical than the others and is primarily for personal inspiration and encouragement to deepen our relationship with God, drawing near to Him so that He might draw near to us. Bible reading, prayer, and perhaps reading a devotional book with a brief message are normally a part of devotions.

Three popular daily devotional booklets are *Our Daily Bread*, *Days of Praise*, and *Today in the Word*. Charles Spurgeon's *Morning and Evening* is a classic devotional tool that gives a message for the beginning of the day and one for the end of the day. Another classic is *My Utmost for His Highest* by Oswald Chambers.

Meditation is a normal part of the devotional method. This is the practice of pondering and reflecting on the meaning of God's words and works and their application to our lives. Anyone who has received a letter from a loved one who is far away understands the meaning of meditation. We read and reread the contents and then think about them. The psalmist said, "I will meditate on Your precepts, and contemplate Your ways" (Psalm 119:15).

Our meditation hopefully carries on throughout the day as we consider how God's Word applies to our particular daily activities. Blessing waits for those who delight in the law of the Lord and meditate on it day and night (Psalm 1:2).

Meditation can be greatly aided by memorization of God's Word. Being able to retrieve scripture from memory is useful when we're discouraged; we're able to ponder the uplifting promises of God. "I remembered Your judgments of old, O Lord, and have comforted myself" (Psalm 119:52).

When facing temptation like the Lord Jesus in Matthew 4, we use scripture that we have learned to be able to remain faithful. The psalmist said, "Your word I have hidden in my heart, that I might not sin against You" (Psalm 119:11).

Being a good witness to those who don't know the Lord requires being able to recall appropriate gospel verses that will be spiritually helpful to them. Many believers have said to themselves following conversations with an unbeliever, "Oh, I wish I would have remembered that particular verse!" They're referring to verses they knew about that would have been helpful in the conversation but that they had never committed to memory.

The devotional method of study prepares us to meet each day with the knowledge that we have been redeemed by Christ and that He'll strengthen us to do His will.

READING THROUGH THE BIBLE

Having recommended six types of Bible study, I want to conclude this chapter by mentioning one more study activity that's advisable: reading through the Bible.

Bible reading should be an ongoing activity in the Christian life. I admire Christians who read through the Bible in one year, something I've never accomplished because I'm easily sidetracked by issues I come across in the text and prefer to investigate at that time. The result is I get behind in my reading schedule. My first attempt to read through the Bible took me five years. That's a lot of rabbit trails! My second time through the Bible took three years. So far, this has been my best attempt. If we have the attitude of Job, we'll stay in God's Word no matter how long it takes us to get through it. He said, "I have treasured the words of His mouth more than my necessary food" (Job 23:12).

Remember, the *activity* of Bible study is more important than the *method*, but learning to use these methods opens doors to discovering the great truths of scripture. As they say at Nike, "Just do it!"

4. COLLABORATION
Using Bible Study Helps

Bring the cloak that I left with Carpus at Troas when
you come—and the books, especially the parchments.
2 TIMOTHY 4:13

Paul, as a Pharisee and as a Christian preacher, was a great student of scripture. No one actually knows what books he was asking Timothy to bring to him when he wrote. But there's a possibility that they were more than books of scripture, that they were books to help him in his own study of scripture.

In this chapter, I'll recommend Bible study tools that are helpful for "a worker" (2 Timothy 2:15). Every worker needs tools of the trade to do his job. The toolbox of Bible students is a personal library, and their tools are study books and helps that aid them in understanding the scriptures. The workshop is that special location where they study.

Study resources produced by Bible scholars give Christians the advantage of reading the insights that these servants of Christ have gained through their own study. Study books are valuable, but they must be kept in their place. They aren't inspired by God as scripture is. They aren't the final word on any biblical text. Our primary source of truth is the Bible. *Sola scriptura* was the Latin saying established during the Protestant Reformation that means "the Bible alone." By using that pronouncement, the Reformers established the Word of God as their only authority for doctrine and practice. God's Word is to be given its rightful place in our lives.

It has been my conviction that when Christians meet to worship and study on the Lord's Day, the Bible should be opened and taught. On rare occasions, I've been in places where a Sunday school manual has been opened in a class and then discussed while Bibles remained closed (though not mine, by the way). This kind of activity doesn't give the Bible its rightful place of priority in a public setting. Whether it's a public or private setting, we shouldn't give our study tools more attention than we give our Bible.

Christians must also beware of becoming *-ites*. These are believers who automatically accept everything that a certain Christian author says or writes. Using the names of popular contemporary Christian authors, these people could be known as Swindollites, Lucadoites, or LaHayeites.

This is an old problem addressed by even the apostle Paul when he asked the Corinthian church, "For when one says, 'I am of Paul,' and another, 'I am of Apollos,' are you not carnal?" (1 Corinthians 3:4). We all have our favorite authors, but they should quickly make this same point, to not become followers of human beings. The words of people must always be confirmed as being true and not just accepted because of who is saying it.

Some Christians have debated whether study books should even be used at all. They believe that only the Bible itself should be studied.

As a young, impressionable believer, I remember listening to a debate between two Christians in the church I attended who took opposing views on this. One said that God speaks only by His Spirit through the Bible and no study books should be used. This sounded very spiritual. The other believed that God could also use study books to be an aid to our better understanding of His Word. Who's right?

My wife and I now own over six hundred study books in our personal library. The Bible-only view is an attractive one economically, but I don't believe it's correct, because as stated earlier, God has gifted certain believers with the gift of teaching. This isn't referring to just a natural ability to teach others. This is a supernatural enablement given by God after salvation (1 Corinthians 12:11, 28).

The gifted teacher can minister through speaking and writing. The mode of getting the information isn't the issue. God uses mature believers to disciple other believers through direct contact in one-to-one or small-group interaction, and indirect contact through the printed page, tapes, CDs, and so on.

None of these resources eliminates the need for spending plenty of time in the Bible. Let's look at some available resources that can help us with our study of the Bible. Please note that the titles I mention are of books that I've used—some may now be out of print or updated under slightly different titles, but all are likely available from libraries, bookstores, or sellers of used books.

BIBLE STUDY HELPS

Study Bibles

As a new believer being invited to a home Bible class, I was amazed to see people with Bibles that had a wealth of additional study notes in them. I had never seen anything like them. I soon purchased a *New Scofield Reference Bible*. When this wore out years later, my next one was a *Ryrie Study Bible*. My wife uses a *MacArthur Study Bible*. Other people I know use the *Life Application Study Bible*. These are only a few in a long list of study Bibles now available in a variety of English translations.

One thing to remember is that the notes in study Bibles are the explanatory words of people, not the authoritative words of God. The study aids are provided as immediate helps and are not meant to be the end of our investigation. We shouldn't depend too heavily on just the explanations in our study Bibles. They'll have helpful introductions to each book of the Bible and outlines so we can see how books fit together. Explanatory notes about the text, doctrine, and Christian living appear on every page. Some study Bibles have charts, articles, extensive cross-references, a concordance, a topical index, and numerous maps.

Bible Dictionaries and Encyclopedias

Among the first tools we need are Bible dictionaries and encyclopedias. They have more than just the definitions of words. They contain brief articles on major Bible subjects with helpful explanations and scripture references related to the subject. These books cover a spectrum of subjects from A to Z, making them a reference tool that gets used repeatedly. I recommend *The New Unger's Bible Dictionary*, *Zondervan's Pictorial Bible Dictionary*, and *The International Standard Bible Encyclopedia*, a five-volume set.

Exhaustive Concordances

An exhaustive concordance lists every reference where every biblical word is found. When you can remember only a few words of a verse, you can look up one of the words and this book helps you find its reference. Often, in the back, you'll also find an English dictionary for Old Testament Hebrew words and New Testament Greek words. It's important to make sure the concordance you use is keyed to the Bible translation you use. *The Strong's Exhaustive Concordance* is keyed to the King James Version. After my Bible, I use this tool more than any other resource that I have.

Topical Bibles

Topical Bibles list biblical words alphabetically and give select references to where the word you are looking for is found. Many times the entire verse is written out so you can read the verse in the book. Larger subjects are broken down into subcategories so you can find verses with a particular emphasis. For example, in *Nave's Topical Bible*, the word *faith* has the following subheadings: faith enjoined; faith exemplified; faith in Christ; the trial of faith. Use this resource when you're doing word studies or character sketches.

Expository Dictionaries

When studying words of the Bible, use an expository dictionary. A Webster's English dictionary is fine as far as it goes, but it primarily deals with English. We're dealing with English translations of Greek words when we study the New Testament. This study aid examines the original Greek words used in verses and then gives a brief definition and explanation of the word. It also has select references to where the Greek word appears in the New Testament. I recommend *The Expository Dictionary of Old and New Testament Words* by W. E. Vine.

Bible Atlases

For those who want a more detailed description of geography in the Bible with explanatory articles, this is the book to use. Atlases contain many more maps than those that appear in the backs of Bibles. This resource won't be used as frequently as others, but it helps to better understand locations and travel in Bible times.

Commentaries

This is my favorite category of study helps. Most of the books I own are commentaries. Using these books is like being taught by great men and women of God.

Some are expository in nature, explaining individual verses and analyzing how they fit together. These generally include an outline of the entire book of the Bible.

Other commentaries are more devotional, emphasizing lessons for Christian living.

Some are technical in nature, working closely with the original languages.

After you read several commentaries, you'll soon discover that the books with more pages are normally more helpful because they address more issues. Difficult questions that arise are usually addressed, including possible solutions.

A personal benefit from reading commentaries written by Bible scholars is that you're able to test your own conclusions against what the experts are saying. This obviously requires that you interact with the Bible text yourself before consulting a commentary. Remember, we're learning how to study the Bible, not learning how to study commentaries.

Commentaries aren't the final word about any text. Even Bible scholars disagree at times. My humble experience has been that I find myself not agreeing with any Bible commentator one hundred percent of the time. My guess is that this is the conclusion of most serious students of the Bible.

Books that have been helpful to me are single books that cover the entire Bible like *Jamieson, Fausset, and Brown Commentary on the Whole Bible* (that's one book!). Sets that cover the entire New Testament or the entire Bible (which provide greater detail) include the six-volume set of Matthew Henry commentaries; *The Bible Knowledge Commentary* by Walvoord and Zuck, a two-volume set; and *The Bible Exposition Commentary* by Warren Wiersbe, a six-volume set. Much larger sets are *The New Testament Commentary* series by Hendriksen and Kistemaker and the *MacArthur New Testament Commentary* series.

One of the first things to find out about authors is their theological persuasion. Some write from a dispensational perspective while others write from the reformed perspective. This is good to know ahead of time because there are doctrinal differences in the content of the books. Your pastor should be able to help with this and make suggestions about what to buy.

Recorded Sermons

Sermons are available on cassettes, CDs, and online. Listening to sermons is a way to increase your knowledge by using undirected time. If you spend a lot of time traveling and aren't using the time for other things, you can listen to hours of Bible messages. You can also listen to Bible teachers while you're taking care of projects in your home or yard.

GETTING BIBLE STUDY RESOURCES

I want to say a few things about where to get Bible study tools. Every Christian should own a few basic study books. To develop your personal library, make a wish list of the books you need. I've learned the hard way not to buy books I'm not acquainted with. The money I used to buy ten books that weren't that good could have been used to buy one good book. Add the study tools to your library that are valuable to you. Get recommendations from Christians who you believe can help you with this project and then visit your local Christian bookstore or an Internet bookseller.

You can also borrow Bible study books from your church library or even many public libraries. If the public library lacks a title you're seeking, it might be able to order the book from another library.

The Internet offers a wealth of free Bible study tools. People frequently comment that when they get on the Internet they use up so much time—if this is your case, you might want to use that time for studying the Bible online.

Here's a list of Web sites in random order with brief descriptions. There is much more on these sites than what's in the descriptions. There are also links to other Bible study sites. When you find a Web site that's helpful to you, put the link into a Bible study file in your FAVORITES so you can visit the site repeatedly.

bible.org

You'll find articles by topic or by passage. They have online Bible dictionaries, concordances, encyclopedias, and an extensive question-and-answer section. Under NAVIGATION click on SITE MAP. Then click on LINKS TO OTHER SITES to find a multitude of Christian Web sites referenced.

crosswalk.com

Under RESOURCES click on BIBLE STUDY TOOLS for commentaries, concordances, dictionaries, and encyclopedias.

studylight.org

Scroll down the left column to Study Resources to find daily devotionals, commentaries, concordances, dictionaries, and sermon helps.

preceptaustin.org

Click on SITE INDEX for an alphabetical listing of this entire Web site. Type any Bible word into the search box to find numerous articles about the word. Bible commentaries with verse-by-verse exposition, dictionaries, and maps are available.

ccel.org

CCEL stands for the Christian Classics Ethereal Library. Click on the SEARCH tab to search by Bible references, by classic Christian author, and by definitions for biblical words.

biblebb.com

Here you'll find sermons and articles by great preachers from the past, MacArthur commentaries, and a lengthy question-and-answer list.

rbc.org

This is the Web site of Radio Bible Class Ministries. Click on BIBLE STUDY for a drop-down menu of various subjects and materials. Continue to click on links until you find the subject you're searching for.

All of these Bible study resources will be helpful in your personal study.

GETTING ORGANIZED

My last suggestion is that you save and file your own notes from your study of the scriptures. Get two three-ring binders to hold your study notes. One notebook can be used for study notes by Bible topics, and the other one can be used for study notes by Bible references. It's a blessing to see and read later what God has taught you in your own study of His Word.

5. MOTIVATION
Putting Thoughts into Action

You therefore, beloved, knowing this beforehand, be on your guard so that you are not carried away by the error of unprincipled men and fall from your own steadfastness, but grow in the grace and knowledge of our Lord and Savior Jesus Christ. To Him be the glory, both now and to the day of eternity. Amen.
2 PETER 3:17–18 NASB

The following ad appeared in the South Central Telephone Company Yellow Pages: "Born to be battered. . .the loving phone call book. Underline it, circle things, write in the margins, turn down page corners—the more you use it, the more valuable it gets to be."

If that's true of a phone book, think how much truer it is of God's Word!

Many people have made their Bibles "personal" by the comments they've written in them year after year. It's hard for some people to think about replacing their old Bibles with new ones even if they're falling apart—because they've found such wisdom, comfort, and power in the pages they've studied and cherished for years.

Alan Redpath, the pastor of Moody Church in Chicago from 1953 to 1962, advised believers to "wreck" their Bibles every ten years. He meant to wear them out by constant use. I once saw a message on a church sign that read, "A Bible that is falling apart is usually owned by someone who isn't." This is a point well taken.

I imagine most believers would say that reading and studying the Bible is a good thing to do. Virtually all Christian families in the United States own at least one Bible. The Bible is repeatedly the bestselling book every year. . .but perhaps still one of the least read. Why the disconnect? The answer has both a human dimension and a spiritual one.

HINDRANCES TO BIBLE STUDY

From a human perspective, the busyness of life can keep us from scripture. Sometimes, we can be lazy when it comes to our spiritual health and responsibilities. And sometimes, we simply don't understand how important Bible study actually is.

From a spiritual perspective, sin in our lives can keep us from spending time in the Word. We can lose our spiritual appetite for the knowledge of God. The forces of darkness are doing all they can to keep us from studying God's truth. Any activity that uses up our time will do—it doesn't have to be evil, just something that weighs us down and takes our time.

We might ask, "Isn't going to church enough? Isn't reading and studying the Bible what pastors and Sunday school teachers do?" It's true that this is a large part of what pastors and teachers are to do, but it's also what everyone in a church congregation is supposed to do. Pastor Alistair Begg has said that his job as a pastor isn't just to feed the sheep, but to teach them how to cook!

Learning God's truth through reading and studying the Bible is something He wants for us. Consider these verses, all of which we've already referenced:

> *Now these [Bereans] were more noble-minded than those in Thessalonica, for they received the word with great eagerness, examining the Scriptures daily to see whether these things were so.*
>
> ACTS 17:11 NASB

For whatever was written in earlier times was written for our instruction.

ROMANS 15:4 NASB

Study to shew thyself approved unto God, a workman that needeth not to be ashamed, rightly dividing the word of truth.

2 TIMOTHY 2:15 KJV

Verses like these should motivate us to be in our Bibles. Believers generally agree that the will of God includes gathering regularly with God's people to worship and pray, living a life of faith and obedience, serving the Lord and spreading His gospel—but how many add that studying the Bible is also the will of God? Is this optional or essential?

As he ended his second letter, the apostle Peter strongly urged believers to "grow. . .in the knowledge of our Lord and Savior Jesus Christ" (2 Peter 3:18), something that starts with knowing His word.

Believers who are growing in knowledge of God's truth have made a conscious decision to study the Word. Seek out those people who know a lot about the Bible, and ask them about their own study habits—then imitate their examples. We are all given the same twenty-four hours a day. You might consider rising earlier in the morning or eliminating a television show or two in the evening. Devote even a small amount of time to Bible study, and add to it as the pursuit becomes a regular habit in your life.

Just like eating, studying the Bible is a lifelong activity. We'll never get to the point where we've learned all that there is to know about God's Word, then be able to stop. Our spirit needs God's Word every day just like our bodies need food.

It's wise to make your study time a matter of prayer. We pray about many things, and this subject is important to Him, too. It's no accident that God allowed you to be born at this time with all the advantages we have to learn His word. Pray about your Bible study every day, because "the prayer of the upright is His delight" (Proverbs 15:8).

Our adversary, the devil, does all he can to keep us from obeying God's will. God wants to bless us, and the devil wants to destroy us. If we as believers fall away from our Bible study, it might seem unimportant to us at the time. But we can be sure that the forces of darkness are celebrating and planning new ways to attack us.

When Jesus defeated Satan's temptation in the wilderness, Luke says, "The devil. . .departed from Him until an opportune time" (Luke 4:13). The devil leaves us for only a brief time. He always returns with different temptations until he finds what's effective against us. Satan knows that Christians, without regular time in the Bible, become weak and ineffective for Christ. But with prayer and the sword of the Spirit—the Word of God—we can overcome this enemy of our souls, enjoying our time with God as we feed on His Word.

God's Goodness

God's goodness should stir us to study His word. His goodness is revealed in our lives in a variety of ways.

The Roman emperor Diocletian persecuted Christians during his reign. In AD 303 he ordered Bibles to be confiscated and burned. Many were destroyed. Today, in countries hostile to the Christian faith, simply owning a Bible is a crime. In our country we have no obstacles like this. Have you ever pondered the blessing that Bibles are legal in our country and so liberally available to us?

The Bible is also available to us in our language. The International Bible Society says the Bible or parts of it have been translated into about twenty-five hundred of the world's sixty-five hundred languages. The majority of language groups have never read the Bible, and its life-giving words about Jesus Christ, in their own language. It's a sad reality that millions of people still have never heard that blessed name.

In some countries where Bibles are permitted, there aren't enough copies for everyone who wants one. In many places, Bibles are shared by believers so they can each read the Word briefly. In other places, a believer who owns a Bible may be asked to become the pastor of a group simply because no one else has access to the Word.

Imagine the hardship of not having Bibles in our worship services. One of the great joys I have as a Bible teacher is to say, "Let's open our Bibles together." Because of the goodness of God, we don't face the limitations of many fellow Christians around the world. We should acknowledge these blessings by gratefully and faithfully studying the Bible.

Over the years, I've been blessed by numerous men of God, pastors and missionaries, who have exemplified love for and diligent pursuit of the scriptures. I've appreciated people in church congregations who have also had an impact on me. Let me tell you about three of them.

1. The example of Eleanor

A dignified elderly widow, Eleanor, who is now with the Lord, attended multiple church services and home Bible classes each week to hear the word of the Lord being taught. When it came to scripture, she seemed to have the energy of a young person. The Bible was the book of her life. When we talked, we would always end up discussing God's Word.

I'll never forget visiting her home to drop off a few Bible sermons on cassette tape. She mentioned that she was doing a personal study on the Gospel of Mark and showed me the six Bible commentaries that she was working through. I was amazed that she'd go to so much effort in a personal study, but she was serious about learning God's Word. At the time, I was still learning what it meant to love God's Word, and Eleanor's example made me want the same kind of energy and excitement for the Bible.

2. The example of a man who couldn't read

An older gentleman, who crossed my path only momentarily, left a lasting impression. He was a little man who briefly attended the same home Bible class that I did. He was a quaint, soft-spoken man, always dressed in a suit and tie. During discussions, it was obvious that he knew a lot about the Bible.

One night, the teacher asked him to read a verse aloud. He paused, hung his head, and admitted he didn't know how to read. I was stunned, as I'm sure everyone else was, too. How could someone who lacked reading skills know so much about the Bible? Obviously, he'd listened to other people teach the Bible—a lot.

The fact that this man overcame the obstacle of illiteracy and still learned the Bible is what struck me. When people are determined to learn God's Word, He'll provide the help they need.

3. The example of Amy

The third person is a wife and stay-at-home mom named Amy. Where is the mother of three young children going to find the time to study the Bible?

To add to this challenge, Amy's been legally blind since her teen years. Can a person with obvious time restraints and the obstacle of partial blindness still study the Bible? The answer is yes, though it requires a great amount of determination and love for God's Word.

Using a powerful magnifying glass, Amy studies scripture for an entire hour—and at times an hour and a half—while two of her children are at school and her youngest takes a nap. That is the quiet time God has provided for her.

The example of these three believers inspires me. And I'm guessing God has put similar people in your life to serve as examples to you. The apostle Paul once said, "Imitate me, just as I also imitate Christ" (1 Corinthians 11:1). On another occasion he wrote, "Brethren, join in following my example, and note those who so walk, as you have us for a pattern" (Philippians 3:17). Value these kinds of people in your life. Imitate the good that you see in them. Thank God that He has brought them into your life. Pray that you'll be a better Christian for having known them.

MARY AND MARTHA

As we conclude, let's consider the lives of Mary and Martha of Bethany. Mary is a great biblical example of a person whose desire was to be taught by Jesus: Every time she appears in the Bible, she's kneeling before Him. In John 11, she's at His feet in sorrow. In John 12, she's at His feet in adoration. In Luke 10, she's at His feet to learn truth. Mary, the worshiper, wants her soul fed by Jesus—her sister Martha, the worker, wants to feed Jesus.

Mary and Martha had welcomed Jesus into their home. With good intentions, Martha took steps to prepare a meal for the honored guest. Mary is now introduced into the story: "And she had a sister called Mary, who also sat at Jesus' feet and heard His word" (Luke 10:39). Martha was in the kitchen cooking food, and Mary was in the living room, learning from Jesus. Martha, annoyed that Mary wasn't helping with the work, interrupted the Lord, saying, "Lord, do You not care that my sister has left me to serve alone? Therefore tell her to help me" (Luke 10:40).

Jesus, in His divine wisdom, analyzed the situation and told Martha she was filled with unnecessary anxiety that had harmfully affected her priorities. The things she worried about really weren't important. "One thing is needed," Jesus told Martha, "and Mary has chosen that good part, which will not be taken away from her" (Luke 10:42).

Jesus commended Mary for having good priorities, namely, learning the Word of God. Bible expositor G. Campbell Morgan calls this "the one supreme necessity."

Mary's experience was that of being taught by the incarnate Christ. Each of us can experience the blessing of being taught by the risen Christ—by the power of His Holy Spirit, through the study of God's amazing Word.

> *Grow in the grace and knowledge of our Lord and Savior Jesus Christ. To Him be the glory, both now and to the day of eternity. Amen.*
>
> 2 PETER 3:18 NASB

BIBLE

Memory Plan

Pamela L. McQuade

INTRODUCTION

The *Bible Memory Plan* is designed for anyone who wants to memorize the Bible. Fazed by that thought, because you aren't "good at memorizing"? Then this is just the book for you. The plan starts out with short verses and slowly expands to longer passages. Along the way are many tips, including memorization methods and bits of encouragement that make learning easier. Verses are identified by topic, so you can relate them to one another.

To help you keep past verses clear, each week of the plan provides a review section. Once a month, the review section expands to five or six verses. As you go on, feel free to review former memory verses as often as necessary to keep them fresh in your mind.

Already have one of these verses memorized? Go to More Verses to Memorize at the end of the book and choose a verse that isn't already in your mind. Otherwise, this list can be used to continue memorization once you've completed the fifty-two verses here.

WEEK 1

BIBLE MEMORY VERSE

*In the beginning God created
the heaven and the earth.*
GENESIS 1:1 KJV

*In the beginning God created
the heavens and the earth.*
GENESIS 1:1 NIV

*In the beginning God created
the heavens and the earth.*
GENESIS 1:1 NLT

TOPIC

Our God

INSIGHT

These opening words of the Old Testament form the foundation
of our knowledge of God.

TIPS AND ENCOURAGEMENT

- Each week's scripture is quoted from three Bible versions.
  Memorize the one that is most familiar to you or that you
  will be most comfortable using in daily life.

- Read the verse aloud to yourself or whomever you're
  memorizing with. On the first day or two, your goal will
  be to get a feel for the whole verse. Every other day focus
  on memorizing a few words at a time.

- If you are single, you may want to memorize with a
  friend or fellow church member.

- Write out the verse on an index card and use it
  throughout the day to review the verse. Before you start

memorizing, check what you've written against the text to make sure you copied it correctly.

- Some people learn better by sound, while others learn visually. Identify how you learn best and spend most of your time using that kind of method. Later chapters will introduce you to many methods of memorization.

- After you finish your week of memorization, keep one copy of an index card with your memory verse, so you can use it to review the verse in following weeks. Make sure you write the topic on the top of the card, so you can review verses by topic if you want to.

WEEK 2

BIBLE MEMORY VERSE

I can do all things through Christ
which strengtheneth me.
PHILIPPIANS 4:13 KJV

I can do all this through him
who gives me strength.
PHILIPPIANS 4:13 NIV

For I can do everything through Christ,
who gives me strength.
PHILIPPIANS 4:13 NLT

TOPIC

Christian Life

INSIGHT

Whether Paul had much or lacked much, he told the Philippian church he had learned to be content. The apostle trusted in God's strength, not his own.

TIPS AND ENCOURAGEMENT

≡   Choose a calm part of the day to focus on your Bible
    memorization. The fewer interruptions you have, the more
    likely you are to be successful.

≡   Establish a set time when you will memorize the verse
    every day. Spend that time focusing on the verse and its
    meaning. Then review the verse over and over again then
    or throughout the day when you have a few minutes.

≡   Don't forget to memorize the book, chapter, and verse. It
    is irritating to have trouble finding a verse just because
    you forgot to memorize where it's located. And if you are
    witnessing to someone, they are more likely to believe
    your testimony if you really know where the verses are.

≡   It's best to choose one version of the Bible for your memo-
    rization, because changing versions can become confusing.
    But if you do use more than one version, be sure to memo-
    rize the version along with the book, chapter, and verse.

REVIEW

Genesis 1:1

WEEK 3

BIBLE MEMORY VERSE

Thy word is a lamp unto my feet,
and a light unto my path.
PSALM 119:105 KJV

Your word is a lamp for my feet,
a light on my path.
PSALM 119:105 NIV

Your word is a lamp to guide my feet
and a light for my path.
PSALM 119:105 NLT

TOPIC

God's Word

INSIGHT

Psalm 119, the longest chapter in the Bible, is all about God's Word. This verse tells us that God's Word guides our lives. If God thinks His Word is important for believers, how should we respond to it?

TIPS AND ENCOURAGEMENT

= When a verse paints a picture, as this one does, use its images to help you remember it. Visual images of a lamp, feet, a light, and a path can remind you of key parts of the verse.

= Don't just focus on each word when you are memorizing. Consider the meaning of the whole verse, and it will be easier to memorize.

= Be encouraged as you begin to remember portions of your verse. If you get a few words wrong, do not worry. Look at your accomplishments and continue to work on the verse.

= Sometimes a verse may provide encouragement for a situation you are in. Allow this element of God's truth to fill your soul.

= Finish your verse in less than a week? Go back and review the ones you've already memorized. Make it a habit to keep reviewing what you've already done. When you have many verses memorized, it will be a good habit to have developed.

REVIEW

Genesis 1:1
Philippians 4:13

WEEK 4

BIBLE MEMORY VERSE

God is my strength and power:
and he maketh my way perfect.
2 SAMUEL 22:33 KJV

It is God who arms me with strength
and keeps my way secure.
2 SAMUEL 22:33 NIV

God is my strong fortress,
and he makes my way perfect.
2 SAMUEL 22:33 NLT

TOPIC

Our God

INSIGHT

David spoke these words of praise after God delivered him from all his enemies. How is He our strong fortress?

TIPS AND ENCOURAGEMENT

≡ In order to memorize effectively, you'll need to commit time to it. No one else can do this for you — it is your choice. But what is more important than your relationship with God? Because you love Him, make the time to memorize His Word.

≡ While you are memorizing, ask yourself what each verse means and how it relates to your Christian life. You are not memorizing just to have words in your head but to make them part of your faith walk.

≡ If you make mistakes, go back and reread your text aloud. As you repeatedly reread the whole text, you will begin to memorize it unknowingly. At some point, you will look at the text and realize that you have it almost down pat. This is the point at which you want to fine-tune your memorization. Look for words you have trouble remembering and begin to focus on them.

REVIEW

Genesis 1:1
Philippians 4:13
Psalm 119:105

WEEK 5

BIBLE MEMORY VERSE

So then faith cometh by hearing,
and hearing by the word of God.
ROMANS 10:17 KJV

Consequently, faith comes from hearing
the message, and the message is heard
through the word about Christ.
ROMANS 10:17 NIV

So faith comes from hearing, that is,
hearing the Good News about Christ.
ROMANS 10:17 NLT

TOPIC

Faith

INSIGHT

People believe because they've heard the gospel message. How can those who have never heard know Christ? What will help them hear?

TIPS AND ENCOURAGEMENT

- Avoid the temptation to memorize too much too soon. You will have a sense of accomplishment when you get some verses in your head in a short time. If you rush it you may become discouraged and not want to continue.

- If one week contains a verse you have already memorized, replace it with one from the More Verses to Memorize section at the end of the book.

- When you have most of your verse down pat, continue to compare it to the original, in case your memorization is not quite accurate.

- Remind yourself that knowing the Bible well is important to your Christian life. Sharing your faith and encouraging others requires that you have God's Word in your mind.

REVIEW

Genesis 1:1
Philippians 4:13
Psalm 119:105
2 Samuel 22:33

WEEK 6

BIBLE MEMORY VERSE

A soft answer turneth away wrath:
but grievous words stir up anger.
PROVERBS 15:1 KJV

A gentle answer turns away wrath,
but a harsh word stirs up anger.
PROVERBS 15:1 NIV

A gentle answer deflects anger,
but harsh words make tempers flare.
PROVERBS 15:1 NLT

TOPIC

Christian Life

INSIGHT

The book of Proverbs offers practical advice on how to live for God. How can we benefit from it?

TIPS AND ENCOURAGEMENT

≡ Absolutely can't find time to memorize a new verse today? Use your limited time to review the verses you've already memorized. But work on the new verse tomorrow.

≡ Forgetting to carry your memorization card with you? Make sure you have one in your car, wallet, and at work (so you can study it on lunchtime or break time).

≡ If you've memorized all the verses so far, be encouraged. At the end of this week, you'll have six verses memorized and have proved to yourself that you have the commitment to memorize the Word.

REVIEW

Now that you have five verses under your belt, review them all.
Genesis 1:1
Philippians 4:13
Psalm 119:105
2 Samuel 22:33
Romans 10:17

WEEK 7

BIBLE MEMORY VERSE

*Every word of God is pure: he is a shield
unto them that put their trust in him.*
PROVERBS 30:5 KJV

*"Every word of God is flawless; he is a shield
to those who take refuge in him."*
PROVERBS 30:5 NIV

Every word of God proves true. He is a shield
to all who come to him for protection.
PROVERBS 30:5 NLT

TOPIC

God's Word

INSIGHT

Agur the son of Jakeh, who penned this verse, recognized how small his store of wisdom was, compared to God's. He encouraged others to trust in the Lord's every word.

TIPS AND ENCOURAGEMENT

≡ Spend a lot of time on your home computer? If you use the Windows program, you can type your verse into the Marquee screensaver. Read your verse before you move your mouse.

≡ Rewrite your verse every day. Leave copies where you can read them often.

≡ Constantly carry one copy of your verse with you. Review it in the doctor's office, as you wait for a friend, or as you take public transportation.

≡ If you'd like to memorize verses more quickly, you can memorize two verses in a week. When you have finished memorizing the verses here, pick up on the More Verses to Memorize in the back of the book.

REVIEW

Psalm 119:105
2 Samuel 22:33
Romans 10:17
Proverbs 15:1

WEEK 8

BIBLE MEMORY VERSE

*A new commandment I give unto you,
that ye love one another; as I have loved you,
that ye also love one another.*
JOHN 13:34 KJV

*A new command I give you: Love one another.
As I have loved you, so you must love one another.*
JOHN 13:34 NIV

*So now I am giving you a new commandment:
Love each other. Just as I have loved you,
you should love each other.*
JOHN 13:34 NLT

TOPIC

Christian Life

INSIGHT

At the Passover supper Jesus gave this command to His disciples. Following His death, they would need His love as their cohesive force.

TIPS AND ENCOURAGEMENT

≡ Look at the structure of longer verses, which may include parts such as an introduction, main concept, secondary ideas, or conclusion. (Each verse may have all of these or just a few of them.)

≡ Once you've identified the parts of the verse, aim at learning one portion at a time. Focus on the first section of the verse, perhaps up to the first punctuation mark, and memorize six to ten words at a time. Breaking the verse into sections helps you see that the whole verse is made up of easily memorized pieces. Take these pieces and work on them one by one. Read through the whole verse periodically as you are memorizing each portion.

≡ When you have the first section under your belt, you are ready to focus on another. Continue in this manner, memorizing a few more words each day and reviewing the old ones, until you have the whole verse memorized.

≡ When you have memorized each portion of the verse, go over the whole verse, to fix the whole thing in your mind. Focus on any areas you have trouble remembering, and fine-tune those spots.

≡ Speaking to the *Boston Globe*, actress Elizabeth Aspenlieder described how she memorizes her parts:

"It's almost like creating a quilt. I learn a piece, and then I go back over the piece I've just learned and add to it, and then I add another piece, and then I kind of do the stitches around the pieces I've just learned."

REVIEW

2 Samuel 22:33
Romans 10:17
Proverbs 15:1
Proverbs 30:5

WEEK 9

BIBLE MEMORY VERSE

If we confess our sins, he is faithful and just to forgive us our sins, and to cleanse us from all unrighteousness.
1 JOHN 1:9 KJV

If we confess our sins, he is faithful and just and will forgive us our sins and purify us from all unrighteousness.
1 JOHN 1:9 NIV

But if we confess our sins to him, he is faithful
and just to forgive us our sins and to cleanse
us from all wickedness.
1 JOHN 1:9 NLT

TOPIC

Salvation

INSIGHT

God is perfect, and sin separates us from Him. John describes confession's role in our relationship with Him.

TIPS AND ENCOURAGEMENT

≡   Having trouble keeping up with your memorization? Review the memorization tips from earlier chapters. Increasingly focus on the most successful methods as you learn longer verses.

≡   Remind yourself that memorizing scripture not only helps you share your faith, it also brings you encouragement. God can bring His Word to your mind when doubt seeks to slip in, but only if you already have that Word there.

≡   If you find a verse you'd like to memorize, add it to the list of More Verses to Memorize in the back of the book, and work on it when you have finished these. Memorizing the Bible is not a rush job, but a lifelong commitment.

REVIEW

Romans 10:17
Proverbs 15:1
Proverbs 30:5
John 13:34

WEEK 10

BIBLE MEMORY VERSE

For by grace are ye saved through faith;
and that not of yourselves: It is the gift of God: Not of works, lest any
man should boast.
EPHESIANS 2:8–9 KJV

For it is by grace you have been saved,
through faith — and this is not from yourselves,
it is the gift of God — not by works,
so that no one can boast.
EPHESIANS 2:8–9 NIV

God saved you by his grace when you believed. And you can't take credit
for this; it is a gift from God. Salvation is not a reward for the good
things we have done, so none of us can boast about it.
EPHESIANS 2:8–9 NLT

TOPIC

Salvation

INSIGHT

The apostle Paul describes God's gracious salvation, in which
He took sinful humans and gave them new life in Him. We could
never earn this great gift from our Lord.

TIPS AND ENCOURAGEMENT

≡ Do not be intimidated by having to memorize two verses
at a time. Start by reading the whole passage. Then
continue in the way you began, breaking each verse
down into smaller passages to memorize.

≡ If your verse has been put to music, sing it. Download
music to listen to whenever you can, or use a CD. But be
certain the musician has not taken artistic license with the
verse, or you may not be memorizing the verse accurately.

Or make up your own tune for your verse. It does not have to be an award-winning ditty, just something that helps you remember the words. Hum it to yourself throughout the day!

≡ Having trouble with your memorization commitment? Ask yourself why you are memorizing. If it's because you want to impress others, God cannot bless your time with His Word. Focus on the real importance of knowing God's Word by carefully reading Psalm 119. Why does God say it's important to know what He's said?

REVIEW

Proverbs 15:1
Proverbs 30:5
John 13:34
1 John 1:9

WEEK 11

BIBLE MEMORY VERSE

Beloved, let us love one another: for love is of God;
and every one that loveth is born of God, and knoweth God.
1 JOHN 4:7 KJV

Dear friends, let us love one another,
for love comes from God. Everyone who loves
has been born of God and knows God.
1 JOHN 4:7 NIV

Dear friends, let us continue to love one another, for love comes
from God. Anyone who loves is a child of God and knows God.
1 JOHN 4:7 NLT

TOPIC

Christian Life

INSIGHT

Love for God and others is a key part of the Christian life. John points out that we can be known as Christians by our love for one another.

TIPS AND ENCOURAGEMENT

- Try to memorize at a time of day when your mind is alert. If you are tired when you try to memorize, you may find you don't remember much.

- Need more tips or encouragement? Read ahead in that section of the *Bible Memory Plan*.

- Forgetting the verses you previously memorized? Daily write them down on cards again and review them. Make certain you are using the same version you first memorized, so you do not become confused.

REVIEW

Proverbs 30:5
John 13:34
1 John 1:9
Ephesians 2:8–9

WEEK 12

BIBLE MEMORY VERSE

Many are the afflictions of the righteous:
but the LORD delivereth him out of them all.
PSALM 34:19 KJV

The righteous person may have many troubles,
but the LORD delivers him from them all.
PSALM 34:19 NIV

The righteous person faces many troubles,
but the LORD comes to the rescue each time.
PSALM 34:19 NLT

TOPIC

Our God

INSIGHT

When David wrote this psalm he was in the midst of trouble, having been driven out from the protection of the king of Gath. David must have feared that his enemy, King Saul, would destroy him, yet he spoke this praise.

TIPS AND ENCOURAGEMENT

≡ Commit to and protect your memorization time. You may need to change *when* you do it, but don't let the world's cares force you to set it aside.

≡ When you've partly memorized a verse, write out the entire verse and underline any words you are struggling with, then focus on those words.

≡ To encourage yourself, give yourself periodic rewards for accomplishing your memorization goals. When you finish this week, give yourself a three-month reward — go to a special coffee shop or have lunch with a friend. Or buy yourself something that you've always wanted.

REVIEW

Proverbs 15:1
Proverbs 30:5
John 13:34
1 John 1:9
Ephesians 2:8–9
1 John 4:7

WEEK 13

BIBLE MEMORY VERSE

Call unto me, and I will answer thee,
and show thee great and mighty things,
which thou knowest not.
JEREMIAH 33:3 KJV

"Call to me and I will answer you and tell you great and unsearchable
things you do not know."
JEREMIAH 33:3 NIV

"Ask me and I will tell you remarkable secrets you do not know about
things to come."
JEREMIAH 33:3 NLT

TOPIC

Our God

INSIGHT

When Jeremiah was shut up in prison, God gave this promise to
him. What great things has God shown you in your Christian life?

TIPS AND ENCOURAGEMENT

- When you are reviewing a verse from memory, try to
  "see" it as you have written it down and read it from that
  written version.

- Think about times when your memorization helped you.
  Have you spoken to someone about Christ and had the
  words in your mind? Have you thought of a verse and
  known that God is working in your own life?

- As you are memorizing, study these verses, too. Read the
  context of the verse to find out what is happening. Use a
  Bible dictionary, commentary, or other study aids to find
  out more about the passage.

- If you do not have many Bible study tools, seek out some online sites that have them available. You may even want to print out some passages, to help your study. Just be certain any commentaries you study are on target theologically.

REVIEW

1 John 1:9
Ephesians 2:8–9
1 John 4:7
Psalm 34:19

WEEK 14

BIBLE MEMORY VERSE

The fear of the LORD is the beginning of knowledge:
but fools despise wisdom and instruction.
PROVERBS 1:7 KJV

The fear of the LORD is the beginning of knowledge,
but fools despise wisdom and instruction.
PROVERBS 1:7 NIV

Fear of the LORD is the foundation of true knowledge,
but fools despise wisdom and discipline.
PROVERBS 1:7 NLT

TOPIC

Seeking God

INSIGHT

Those who do not fear God will never share in His wisdom. Do not be surprised when others despise Him and your faith.

TIPS AND ENCOURAGEMENT

- If others do not support you in your memorization, be kind to them. Learning the scriptures but offending others is not a good Christian testimony. Work to balance compassion and your commitment to God's Word.

- If your spouse won't memorize with you, prayerfully invite another family member to do so.

- Not a morning person? Maybe you need to memorize in the evening. Everyone's body clock is different. Make the best use of yours.

REVIEW

1 John 1:9
Ephesians 2:8–9
1 John 4:7
Psalm 34:19
Jeremiah 33:3

WEEK 15

BIBLE MEMORY VERSE

*There is therefore now no condemnation to
them which are in Christ Jesus, who walk not after the flesh,
but after the Spirit.*
ROMANS 8:1 KJV

*Therefore, there is now no condemnation
for those who are in Christ Jesus.*
ROMANS 8:1 NIV

*So now there is no condemnation for those
who belong to Christ Jesus.*
ROMANS 8:1 NLT

TOPIC

Salvation

INSIGHT

Though all these versions focus on the salvation Jesus brings to believers, the King James Version follows a later manuscript that adds the last part of the verse.

TIPS AND ENCOURAGEMENT

- Scripture translations may vary slightly, based on the original-language manuscript that was used. Modern translations are more likely to use an earlier manuscript than older translations, like the King James Version. But they often note variations in other manuscripts, as the New International Version does for this verse.

- If you are memorizing without referring to your written text and begin to become confused, stop! Wait until you have your text with you, so you do not have to correct a wrong memorization.

REVIEW

1 John 4:7
Psalm 34:19
Jeremiah 33:3
Proverbs 1:7

WEEK 16

BIBLE MEMORY VERSE

*For I am not ashamed of the gospel of Christ:
for it is the power of God unto salvation to every one that believeth;
to the Jew first, and also to the Greek.*
ROMANS 1:16 KJV

For I am not ashamed of the gospel,
because it is the power of God that brings
salvation to everyone who believes:
first to the Jew, then to the Gentile.
ROMANS 1:16 NIV

For I am not ashamed of this Good News
about Christ. It is the power of God at work,
saving everyone who believes —
the Jew first and also the Gentile.
ROMANS 1:16 NLT

TOPIC

Salvation

INSIGHT

God can work in the lives of those who hear the Good News.
Scripture is designed to save souls, no matter what background
those people come from.

TIPS AND ENCOURAGEMENT

≡ Are you feeling a bit bored with your favorite way of
memorizing? Shake yourself up by doing something
different: plaster your verse on the bathroom mirror or
sing it in the shower while you prepare for your day.
Try some other methods in the Tips and Encouragement
sections that you haven't used before.

≡ Keep working on your quilt of Bible memorization. Are
you making a wall hanging or a real cover for the cold
days in your life? You are the one who decides how much
of the Word you will put in your mind.

REVIEW

Psalm 34:19
Jeremiah 33:3
Proverbs 1:7
Romans 8:1

WEEK 17

BIBLE MEMORY VERSE

But the fruit of the Spirit is love, joy, peace, longsuffering, gentleness, goodness, faith, meekness, temperance: against such there is no law.
GALATIANS 5:22–23 KJV

But the fruit of the Spirit is love, joy, peace, forbearance, kindness, goodness, faithfulness, gentleness and self-control. Against such things there is no law.
GALATIANS 5:22–23 NIV

But the Holy Spirit produces this kind of fruit in our lives: love, joy, peace, patience, kindness, goodness, faithfulness, gentleness, and self-control. There is no law against these things!
GALATIANS 5:22–23 NLT

TOPIC

Christian Life

INSIGHT

Paul pictures believers as bearing the fruit of good works and attitudes in their lives. This is living by the Spirit.

TIPS AND ENCOURAGEMENT

- Make use of the verse you are learning by sharing it with someone else. Quote it, then tell them what it means or how it has affected your life.

- Are you memorizing only a couple of days a week? Recommit yourself to daily memorization by identifying why you aren't being committed and changing whatever gets in the way.

- Remind yourself of the benefits of knowing the Word well.

REVIEW

Jeremiah 33:3
Proverbs 1:7
Romans 8:1
Romans 1:16

WEEK 18

BIBLE MEMORY VERSE

For the preaching of the cross is to them that perish foolishness;
but unto us which are saved it is the power of God.
1 CORINTHIANS 1:18 KJV

For the message of the cross is foolishness to those
who are perishing, but to us who are being saved
it is the power of God.
1 CORINTHIANS 1:18 NIV

The message of the cross is foolish to those who
are headed for destruction! But we who are being
saved know it is the very power of God.
1 CORINTHIANS 1:18 NLT

TOPIC

Salvation

INSIGHT

The cross seems foolish to unbelievers but is the very center of the faith to those who believe. God's wisdom is way beyond the wisdom of man.

TIPS AND ENCOURAGEMENT

- When reviewing verses, put more than one on a file card to carry with you. Use the back of the card, too. That way you won't have a large stack of cards to carry. You can group your verses by topic.

REVIEW

Psalm 34:19
Jeremiah 33:3
Proverbs 1:7
Romans 8:1
Romans 1:16
Galatians 5:22–23

WEEK 19

BIBLE MEMORY VERSE

In the beginning was the Word,
and the Word was with God, and the Word was God.
The same was in the beginning with God.
JOHN 1:1–2 KJV

In the beginning was the Word,
and the Word was with God, and the Word was God.
He was with God in the beginning.
JOHN 1:1–2 NIV

In the beginning the Word already existed.
The Word was with God, and the Word was God.
He existed in the beginning with God.
JOHN 1:1–2 NLT

TOPIC

Our God

INSIGHT

Who is this mysterious Word? It's Jesus (see John 1:14). It's no coincidence that these verses parallel the beginning of Genesis. John is declaring that Jesus is God, and Lord of creation.

TIPS AND ENCOURAGEMENT

- Sometimes review your verses according to topic instead of in the order you've memorized them in. Organize your verses by topic, and review each group separately. This will make review time more interesting and will also give you a firmer grasp on what scripture says about these subjects.

- If a verse seems confusing to you, pick up your Bible and read a few verses around it or even the whole chapter. John 1 is an amazing description of Jesus that appears nowhere else in scripture.

REVIEW

Romans 8:1
Romans 1:16
Galatians 5:22–23
1 Corinthians 1:18

WEEK 20

BIBLE MEMORY VERSE

*Trust in the LORD with all thine heart;
and lean not unto thine own understanding.
In all thy ways acknowledge him,
and he shall direct thy paths.*
PROVERBS 3:5–6 KJV

*Trust in the LORD with all your heart
and lean not on your own understanding;
in all your ways submit to him, and he
will make your paths straight.*
PROVERBS 3:5–6 NIV

*Trust in the LORD with all your heart;
do not depend on your own understanding.
Seek his will in all you do, and he will
show you which path to take.*
PROVERBS 3:5–6 NLT

TOPIC

Faith

INSIGHT

When wise King Solomon gave advice to his son, he encouraged
him to trust in God, not his own wisdom. Even the most astute
human cannot direct a life as well as God can.

TIPS AND ENCOURAGEMENT

≡ What do you know about the people who penned or are
involved in the verses you are memorizing? If you know
that God gave King Solomon great wisdom, but the wise
king advised others to rely on God, this passage has a lot
more meaning.

≡ If you aren't studying the Bible, use these verses to start a
study. Find out as much as you can about each verse. Do
you need to look up some you've already studied?

REVIEW

Romans 1:16
Galatians 5:22–23
1 Corinthians 1:18
John 1:1–2

WEEK 21

BIBLE MEMORY VERSE

*Know ye not that ye are the temple of God,
and that the Spirit of God dwelleth in you?*
1 CORINTHIANS 3:16 KJV

*Don't you know that you yourselves
are God's temple and that God's Spirit
dwells in your midst?*
1 CORINTHIANS 3:16 NIV

Don't you realize that all of you together
are the temple of God and that the
Spirit of God lives in you?
1 CORINTHIANS 3:16 NLT

TOPIC

Christian Life

INSIGHT

Now that there is no earthly temple building, God has made His
people His temple, filling them with His Spirit.

TIPS AND ENCOURAGEMENT

≡ When starting to work on a verse, ask yourself questions
   such as: What does this verse mean to me in my Christian
   life? How would the world be different if this were not
   true? How can this help me in my Christian life?

≡ When you memorize, you are deepening your knowledge
   of God. Don't let your focus be only on memorization
   success but on how you are building your relationship
   with your Lord.

REVIEW

Galatians 5:22–23
1 Corinthians 1:18
John 1:1–2
Proverbs 3:5–6

WEEK 22

BIBLE MEMORY VERSE

I will lift up mine eyes unto the hills,
from whence cometh my help. My help cometh from the LORD,
which made heaven and earth.
PSALM 121:1–2 KJV

I lift up my eyes to the mountains –
where does my help come from?
My help comes from the LORD,
the Maker of heaven and earth.
PSALM 121:1–2 NIV

I look up to the mountains –
does my help come from there?
My help comes from the LORD,
who made heaven and earth!
PSALM 121:1–2 NLT

TOPIC

Our God

INSIGHT

The psalmist glorifies the Lord, who helps and protects His people. Who else can we trust this way?

TIPS AND ENCOURAGEMENT

- Even though you are not memorizing all three versions, read over the translations from the other Bible versions. What insight can you get from the way another translator sees this verse?

- What does this verse teach you about the topic? What other verses have you memorized on this topic? How do they relate to each other?

- Remember to add to the quilt of your Bible memorization each day, piece by piece. Soon you will have a warm blanket that will protect you from the evil one's darts.

REVIEW

1 Corinthians 1:18
John 1:1–2
Proverbs 3:5–6
1 Corinthians 3:16

WEEK 23

BIBLE MEMORY VERSE

But without faith it is impossible to please him:
for he that cometh to God must believe that he is,
and that he is a rewarder of them that diligently seek him.
HEBREWS 11:6 KJV

And without faith it is impossible to please God,
because anyone who comes to him must believe that he
exists and that he rewards those who earnestly seek him.
HEBREWS 11:6 NIV

And it is impossible to please God without faith.
Anyone who wants to come to him must believe that God
exists and that he rewards those who sincerely seek him.
HEBREWS 11:6 NLT

TOPIC

Faith

INSIGHT

This is a portion of the impressive faith chapter of Hebrews, which describes the importance of faith, focusing on the actions of Old Testament believers.

TIPS AND ENCOURAGEMENT

- How can you use this verse in your personal life? When you share your faith with other Christians? When you witness?

- What are the best times in your day for memorization? Are you making the most of them? If you can't memorize at your usual time, are you able to find another patch in your day when you can do it? Be persistent in your memorization.

REVIEW

John 1:1–2
Proverbs 3:5–6
1 Corinthians 3:16
Psalm 121:1–2

WEEK 24

BIBLE MEMORY VERSE

*And we know that all things work together
for good to them that love God, to them who
are the called according to his purpose.*
ROMANS 8:28 KJV

*And we know that in all things God works for
the good of those who love him, who have been
called according to his purpose.*
ROMANS 8:28 NIV

*And we know that God causes everything to work
together for the good of those who love God and
are called according to his purpose for them.*
ROMANS 8:28 NLT

TOPIC

Our God

INSIGHT

In Romans 8 Paul encourages us to look forward to our future in
Christ as the Spirit works in our lives.

TIPS AND ENCOURAGEMENT

≡   What insights have you gotten about God by memorizing
His Word? How is it different from simply reading the
Word?

- Memorization can strengthen you by preparing you for whatever you face in your Christian life. Can you answer the questions of seekers more readily, find encouragement, and withstand temptation when it comes?

REVIEW

1 Corinthians 1:18
John 1:1–2
Proverbs 3:5–6
1 Corinthians 3:16
Psalm 121:1–2
Hebrews 11:6

WEEK 25

BIBLE MEMORY VERSE

*Wherefore, my beloved brethren, let every man
be swift to hear, slow to speak, slow to wrath:
For the wrath of man worketh not the
righteousness of God.*
JAMES 1:19–20 KJV

*My dear brothers and sisters, take note of this:
Everyone should be quick to listen, slow to speak and slow
to become angry, because human anger does not produce
the righteousness that God desires.*
JAMES 1:19–20 NIV

*Understand this, my dear brothers and sisters:
You must all be quick to listen, slow to speak, and slow to get angry.
Human anger does not produce the righteousness God desires.*
JAMES 1:19–20 NLT

TOPIC

Christian Life

INSIGHT

The book of James is rich in wisdom for living the Christian life, including this advice on avoiding anger.

TIPS AND ENCOURAGEMENT

≡ Some portions of the Bible provide highly practical advice on how to live as a Christian. Be encouraged that God provides much information on how to live for Him and with others. Use it!

≡ When you're reviewing verses, don't always take them in the same order. This unexpectedness will help you memorize them more effectively.

REVIEW

1 Corinthians 3:16
Psalm 121:1–2
Hebrews 11:6
Romans 8:28

WEEK 26

BIBLE MEMORY VERSE

Finally, my brethren, be strong in the Lord,
and in the power of his might. Put on the whole armour of God,
that ye may be able to stand against the wiles of the devil.
EPHESIANS 6:10–11 KJV

Finally, be strong in the Lord and in his mighty power.
Put on the full armor of God, so that you can take your
stand against the devil's schemes.
EPHESIANS 6:10–11 NIV

A final word: Be strong in the Lord and in his mighty power.
Put on all of God's armor so that you will be able to
stand firm against all strategies of the devil.
EPHESIANS 6:10–11 NLT

TOPIC

Christian Life

INSIGHT

Paul shows believers that their strength is not in their ability to obey God, but in their Lord's power. Putting on God's armor protects the faithful from all of Satan's wiles. In the following verses, the apostle describes this armor that helps Christians stand strong in the faith.

TIPS AND ENCOURAGEMENT

- Don't forget to carry your scripture cards with you, wherever you go. Going on vacation? Pack them so you can review them on the plane or during a long drive.

- Remember a time when God has reminded you of a scripture you memorized just at the moment when you needed it. Aren't you glad you memorized that verse?

- Congratulations. You are halfway through a year of memorization, if you have kept up with the whole Bible Memory Plan. If it's taken you more than half of a year, you may not have been speedy, but you were faithful.

REVIEW

Psalm 121:1–2
Hebrews 11:6
Romans 8:28
James 1:19–20

WEEK 27

BIBLE MEMORY VERSE

Humble yourselves therefore under the mighty hand of God, that he may exalt you in due time: Casting all your care upon him; for he careth for you.
1 PETER 5:6–7 KJV

Humble yourselves, therefore, under God's mighty hand,
that he may lift you up in due time. Cast all your
anxiety on him because he cares for you.
1 PETER 5:6–7 NIV

So humble yourselves under the mighty power
of God, and at the right time he will lift you
up in honor. Give all your worries and cares
to God, for he cares about you.
1 PETER 5:6–7 NLT

TOPIC

Seeking God

INSIGHT

God is not trying to develop believers' pride. Though we don't like the idea of being humble, it is part of the Christian portfolio. When we are humble, we allow God to control our lives and futures.

TIPS AND ENCOURAGEMENT

≡ How have you been blessed by your memorization? Share this with a Christian friend whom you can encourage to start memorizing, too.

≡ When you first started memorizing, was it hard for you? How has practice made it easier for you?

REVIEW

Hebrews 11:6
Romans 8:28
James 1:19–20
Ephesians 6:10–11

WEEK 28

BIBLE MEMORY VERSE

Who can find a virtuous woman?
For her price is far above rubies.
The heart of her husband doth safely trust in her,
so that he shall have no need of spoil.
PROVERBS 31:10–11 KJV

A wife of noble character who can find?
She is worth far more than rubies.
Her husband has full confidence in
her and lacks nothing of value.
PROVERBS 31:10–11 NIV

Who can find a virtuous and capable wife?
She is more precious than rubies.
Her husband can trust her,
and she will greatly enrich his life.
PROVERBS 31:10–11 NLT

TOPIC

Christian Life

INSIGHT

King Lemuel's mother gave him this wise advice on marriage.
Many believers have discovered the wisdom of such a union.

TIPS AND ENCOURAGEMENT

≡ Even when you think you have the verse well
memorized, periodically check yourself against the
written text, until you have it down perfectly.

≡ Continue repeating a verse, even after you have
memorized it. Otherwise, it's easy to forget. Try to make
the verse a part of your everyday life. Think of it when
you are driving, running an errand, or before you fall
asleep at night.

REVIEW

Romans 8:28
James 1:19–20
Ephesians 6:10–11
1 Peter 5:6–7

WEEK 29

BIBLE MEMORY VERSE

*Come now, and let us reason together,
saith the LORD: though your sins be as scarlet,
they shall be as white as snow; though they
be red like crimson, they shall be as wool.*
ISAIAH 1:18 KJV

*"Come now, let us settle the matter,"
says the LORD. "Though your sins are like scarlet,
they shall be as white as snow; though they are
red as crimson, they shall be like wool."*
ISAIAH 1:18 NIV

*"Come now, let's settle this," says the LORD.
"Though your sins are like scarlet, I will make
them as white as snow. Though they are red like
crimson, I will make them as white as wool."*
ISAIAH 1:18 NLT

TOPIC

Salvation

INSIGHT

Through the prophet Isaiah, God called His people to turn from their sin and obey Him. Only God can cleanse sin until it's snow white.

TIPS AND ENCOURAGEMENT

≡   When you have memorized verses on salvation, share
    them lovingly with those who do not know God.
    Remember, if you use a verse in anger against someone,
    you are unlikely to win that soul to Christ.

≡   What other verses about salvation would you like to
    memorize? Add them to the More Verses to Memorize
    section at the back of the book.

REVIEW

James 1:19–20
Ephesians 6:10–11
1 Peter 5:6–7
Proverbs 31:10–11

WEEK 30

BIBLE MEMORY VERSE

*If ye then be risen with Christ, seek those things
which are above, where Christ sitteth on the right hand of God.
Set your affection on things above, not on things on the earth.*
COLOSSIANS 3:1–2 KJV

*Since, then, you have been raised with Christ, set your
hearts on things above, where Christ is, seated at the right hand of God.
Set your minds on things above, not on earthly things.*
COLOSSIANS 3:1–2 NIV

*Since you have been raised to new life with Christ,
set your sights on the realities of heaven, where Christ
sits in the place of honor at God's right hand.
Think about the things of heaven, not the things of earth.*
COLOSSIANS 3:1–2 NLT

TOPIC

Seeking God

INSIGHT

Paul encourages Christians to take their new life in Christ seriously and turn aside from worldly ways.

TIPS AND ENCOURAGEMENT

≡ To be certain you know the chapter and verse for your verses, sometimes begin with the chapter and verse; then try to say the verse aloud. That way you'll know you are certain where each verse comes from.

≡ If a verse does not seem critical to your spiritual life today, memorize it for future reference. God gave us the whole Bible for a purpose, and you never know when a verse will be important to you.

REVIEW

Romans 8:28
James 1:19–20
Ephesians 6:10–11
1 Peter 5:6–7
Proverbs 31:10–11
Isaiah 1:18

WEEK 31

BIBLE MEMORY VERSE

But they that wait upon the LORD shall renew their strength;
they shall mount up with wings
as eagles; they shall run, and not be weary;
and they shall walk, and not faint.
ISAIAH 40:31 KJV

But those who hope in the LORD will renew
their strength. They will soar on wings like eagles;
they will run and not grow weary, they will walk and not be faint.
ISAIAH 40:31 NIV

*But those who trust in the L*ORD *will find new strength.*
They will soar high on wings like eagles. They will run
and not grow weary. They will walk and not faint.
ISAIAH 40:31 NLT

TOPIC

Our God

INSIGHT

Isaiah describes how believers who depend on the everlasting, all-powerful God can rely on His strength.

TIPS AND ENCOURAGEMENT

≡ Don't stop writing down your memory verse every day. Having trouble remembering the verses you memorized early on? Write them down for a few days, too, until you have them down pat again.

≡ Having trouble remembering which verse goes with which reference? Write down all your verses on a file card and cut off the references with a paper cutter. Then match them up again. Or play a game with your family, having everyone draw verses or references from a pile. Lay out the other cards flat on a table, where they all can be seen and take turns matching the verses and references. Whoever first matches the pulled verses correctly wins.

≡ Is memorizing the Word more exciting now than when you started? What have you learned from doing this?

REVIEW

1 Peter 5:6–7
Proverbs 31:10–11
Isaiah 1:18
Colossians 3:1–2

WEEK 32

BIBLE MEMORY VERSE

Verily, verily, I say unto you, he that heareth
my word, and believeth on him that sent me,
hath everlasting life, and shall not come into
condemnation; but is passed from death unto life.
JOHN 5:24 KJV

"Very truly I tell you, whoever hears my word
and believes him who sent me has eternal life and
will not be judged but has crossed over from death to life."
JOHN 5:24 NIV

"I tell you the truth, those who listen to my
message and believe in God who sent me have
eternal life. They will never be condemned for
their sins, but they have already passed
from death into life."
JOHN 5:24 NLT

TOPIC

Salvation

INSIGHT

Here Jesus describes His role in salvation as He fulfills the Father's will. No one can know God and fail to know His Son.

TIPS AND ENCOURAGEMENT

≡   How has your spiritual life benefited from memorizing scripture? Are you more confident in your Christian walk? How have you been able to help others because you know the Word?

≡   Why is God's Word so important to believers and for those who have yet to believe?

- ≡ What goals do you need to set for your Bible memorization plan? What would you like to accomplish when you've finished this book?

REVIEW

Proverbs 31:10–11
Isaiah 1:18
Colossians 3:1–2
Isaiah 40:31

WEEK 33

BIBLE MEMORY VERSE

God is our refuge and strength, a very present help in trouble.
Therefore will not we fear, though the earth be removed, and though
the mountains be carried into the midst of the sea.
PSALM 46:1–2 KJV

God is our refuge and strength, an ever-present help in trouble.
Therefore we will not fear, though the earth give way
and the mountains fall into the heart of the sea.
PSALM 46:1–2 NIV

God is our refuge and strength, always ready to help
in times of trouble. So we will not fear when earthquakes
come and the mountains crumble into the sea.
PSALM 46:1–2 NLT

TOPIC

Our God

INSIGHT

The psalmist describes God as our fortress and the one who provides us with refuge from all our troubles.

TIPS AND ENCOURAGEMENT

- Use the word-picture of God as a fortress to help you memorize this verse. How has God been a fortress in your life?

- Are you still using file cards to help memorize your verses? You may want to keep the older cards in a box or other container that you can have them handy when you need to review them.

REVIEW

Isaiah 1:18
Colossians 3:1–2
Isaiah 40:31
John 5:24

WEEK 34

BIBLE MEMORY VERSE

The LORD also will be a refuge for the oppressed, a refuge in times of trouble. And they that know thy name will put their trust in thee: for thou, LORD, hast not forsaken them that seek thee.
PSALM 9:9–10 KJV

The LORD is a refuge for the oppressed, a stronghold in times of trouble. Those who know your name will trust in you, for you, LORD, have never forsaken those who seek you.
PSALM 9:9–10 NIV

The LORD is a shelter for the oppressed, a refuge in times of trouble. Those who know your name trust in you, for you, O LORD, do not abandon those who search for you.
PSALM 9:9–10 NLT

Topic

Our God

Insight

As David recounts God's wonderful deeds, he speaks of God's protection of His people and calls believers to worship Him.

Tips and Encouragement

- When scripture has numerous verses on the same topic, God's telling us this is an important concept. How is this verse similar to the one you memorized last week? What does each tell you about God?

- Many Bible verses, like this one, are intensely personal. What does it tell you about God's love for you?

Review

Colossians 3:1–2
Isaiah 40:31
John 5:24
Psalm 46:1–2

WEEK 35

BIBLE MEMORY VERSE

For the word of God is quick, and powerful,
and sharper than any twoedged sword, piercing even to the dividing
asunder of soul and spirit, and of the joints and marrow, and is a
discerner of the thoughts and intents of the heart.
HEBREWS 4:12 KJV

For the word of God is alive and active.
Sharper than any double-edged sword,
it penetrates even to dividing soul and spirit, joints and marrow; it
judges the thoughts
and attitudes of the heart.
HEBREWS 4:12 NIV

For the word of God is alive and powerful.
It is sharper than the sharpest two-edged sword, cutting between soul
and spirit, between joint and marrow. It exposes our innermost
thoughts and desires.
HEBREWS 4:12 NLT

TOPIC

God's Word

INSIGHT

God's Word convicts people of their sin and shows them how
their lives cannot live up to His commandments. Even those
who have come to faith in God are constantly shown their own
inability to live for Him, apart from His empowerment.

TIPS AND ENCOURAGEMENT

≡ As you memorize longer verses, do not be intimidated
by the length of any verse. Begin by reading it over a few
more times in the first day or two of your memorization.
You may break it down into each sentence and focus on
them singly. In this case, if you simply read the verse over

and over for a couple of days, then memorize about nine words a day, you will easily have it all memorized in a week.

≡   How much have you learned about God from memorizing His Word? Review past verses to remind yourself how He has led you.

REVIEW

Isaiah 40:31
John 5:24
Psalm 46:1–2
Psalm 9:9–10

WEEK 36

BIBLE MEMORY VERSE

I am crucified with Christ: nevertheless I live;
yet not I, but Christ liveth in me: and the life which I now live in the
flesh I live by the faith of the Son of God, who loved me,
and gave himself for me.
GALATIANS 2:20 KJV

I have been crucified with Christ and I no longer live, but Christ lives in
me. The life I now live in the body, I live by faith in the Son of God,
who loved me and gave himself for me.
GALATIANS 2:20 NIV

My old self has been crucified with Christ. It is no longer I who live, but
Christ lives in me. So I live in this earthly body by trusting in the Son of
God, who loved me and gave himself for me.
GALATIANS 2:20 NLT

TOPIC

Salvation

INSIGHT

In saving us, Jesus is not simply making us better but creating totally new people, whose sinful lives have died with Him. God lives in our hearts because of His sacrifice.

TIPS AND ENCOURAGEMENT

≡ Some verses powerfully impact us as we read them. We may be encouraged to live for Christ more powerfully or we may feel discouraged, thinking we can never accomplish this. Either way, we need to trust in God's power to work in our lives.

≡ Has this verse become so commonplace in your life that you fail to respond to it? Think back to the days when you were a very young Christian. What would it have meant to you then? How did your life change?

REVIEW

Colossians 3:1–2
Isaiah 40:31
John 5:24
Psalm 46:1–2
Psalm 9:9–10
Hebrews 4:12

WEEK 37

BIBLE MEMORY VERSE

Blessed is the man that walketh not in the counsel of the ungodly, nor standeth in the way of sinners, nor sitteth in the seat of the scornful. But his delight is in the law of the LORD; and in his law doth he meditate day and night.
PSALM 1:1–2 KJV

Blessed is the one who does not walk in step with the wicked or stand in the way that sinners take or sit in the company of mockers, but whose delight is in the law of the LORD, and who meditates on his law day and night.
PSALM 1:1–2 NIV

Oh, the joys of those who do not follow the advice of the wicked, or stand around with sinners, or join in with mockers. But they delight in the law of the LORD, meditating on it day and night.
PSALM 1:1–2 NLT

TOPIC

Seeking God

INSIGHT

Psalm 1 compares the blessed person, or believer, to the wicked, or unbelieving, one. Though the world says otherwise, scripture tells us that trusting in God makes for a joyful life.

TIPS AND ENCOURAGEMENT

≡   Standing up against sin may not always seem blessed, yet we believe in God's Word and eventually find that it is true. Have you found yourself doubting the truth of God's Word, only to have it prove itself in your eyes?

≡   What encourages you most to memorize God's Word? Is it seeing the way it works in your life, the joy you have in knowing God more deeply, or the impact it has on others when you share it? Focus on whatever encourages you to memorize if you just don't feel like spending time doing it. Make it your goal to share God's truth with others.

REVIEW

Psalm 46:1–2
Psalm 9:9–10
Hebrews 4:12
Galatians 2:20

WEEK 38

BIBLE MEMORY VERSE

Give, and it shall be given unto you;
good measure, pressed down, and shaken together, and running over,
shall men give into your bosom. For with the same measure that ye mete
withal it shall be measured to you again.
LUKE 6:38 KJV

"Give, and it will be given to you. A good measure, pressed down,
shaken together and running over, will be poured into your lap.
For with the measure you use, it will be measured to you."
LUKE 6:38 NIV

"Give, and you will receive. Your gift will return to you in
full — pressed down, shaken together to make room for more,
running over, and poured into your lap. The amount you
give will determine the amount you get back."
LUKE 6:38 NLT

TOPIC

Christian Life

INSIGHT

Though Christians often use this verse to encourage monetary giving, in context, it is talking about judging others. Forgive, and you will also be forgiven when you sin.

TIPS AND ENCOURAGEMENT

≡ Are you making use of these verses in your own life and attempting to understand them better? Do not allow your memorization to become rote learning, but interact with the verses day by day.

≡ Are you using these verses to help you understand and help others? The Word of God should be having an impact on your Christian walk, not just on your spiritual understanding of the relationship between yourself and God.

REVIEW

Psalm 9:9–10
Hebrews 4:12
Galatians 2:20
Psalm 1:1–2

WEEK 39

BIBLE MEMORY VERSE

All scripture is given by inspiration of God,
and is profitable for doctrine, for reproof,
for correction, for instruction in righteousness: That the man of God
may be perfect, thoroughly furnished unto all good works.
2 TIMOTHY 3:16–17 KJV

All Scripture is God-breathed and is useful for teaching, rebuking,
correcting and training in righteousness, so that the servant of God may
be thoroughly equipped for every good work.
2 TIMOTHY 3:16–17 NIV

All Scripture is inspired by God and is useful to teach us what is true
and to make us realize what is wrong in our lives. It corrects us when we
are wrong and teaches us to do what is right.
God uses it to prepare and equip his people
to do every good work.
2 TIMOTHY 3:16–17 NLT

TOPIC

God's Word

INSIGHT

Paul pointed to Timothy's lifelong acquaintance with scripture
as the source of this young man's wisdom in spiritual things.
Through His Word, God had equipped the young pastor to lead a
congregation.

TIPS AND ENCOURAGEMENT

≡ It can be spiritually challenging to take the Word at its word. We don't have to be Christians for long before we understand that scripture is both an encouragement and a challenge. Though we may not like God's correction in our lives, it is an important part of our spiritual walks. How we accept it tells a lot about our spiritual maturity. None of us are perfect, but God is perfecting our lives through His Spirit.

≡ How well equipped are you as a believer? As a leader? How can memorization help you to be better equipped?

≡ When you have almost finished memorizing a verse, do you go back over the whole verse again, to make sure you have memorized it correctly? It's easy to slip up on memorization when you think you have it down pat.

REVIEW

Hebrews 4:12
Galatians 2:20
Psalm 1:1–2
Luke 6:38

WEEK 40

BIBLE MEMORY VERSE

Ask, and it shall be given you; seek, and ye shall find; knock, and it shall be opened unto you: For every one that asketh receiveth; and he that seeketh findeth; and to him that knocketh it shall be opened.
MATTHEW 7:7–8 KJV

"Ask and it will be given to you; seek and you will find; knock and the door will be opened to you. For everyone who asks receives; the one who seeks finds; and to the one who knocks, the door will be opened."
MATTHEW 7:7–8 NIV

"Keep on asking, and you will receive what you ask for. Keep on seeking, and you will find. Keep on knocking, and the door will be opened to you. For everyone who asks, receives. Everyone who seeks, finds. And to everyone who knocks, the door will be opened."
MATTHEW 7:7–8 NLT

TOPIC

Seeking God

INSIGHT

In these verses God isn't promising that every Christian will have an unending succession of luxuries, but that He will give believers the good things they truly need. When we have a real need and seek God persistently, we can count on Him to provide.

TIPS AND ENCOURAGEMENT

≡ When you memorize a verse, make certain you know what it really means. Otherwise, you may end up sharing the verse but not conveying its real meaning to another person. If necessary, pick up your Bible and read the surrounding verses.

≡ If you share a verse, and another Christian sparks a heated debate with you on its meaning, you may want to spend some time in the scripture and in Bible commentaries to be sure you understand the Word properly. Too much heated debate without knowledge leads to division, not real understanding.

REVIEW

Galatians 2:20
Psalm 1:1–2
Luke 6:38
2 Timothy 3:16–17

WEEK 41

BIBLE MEMORY VERSE

*Be careful for nothing; but in every thing by prayer and
supplication with thanksgiving let your requests be
made known unto God. And the peace of God, which passeth
all understanding, shall keep your hearts and
minds through Christ Jesus.*
PHILIPPIANS 4:6–7 KJV

*Do not be anxious about anything, but in every situation,
by prayer and petition, with thanksgiving, present your requests to God.
And the peace of God, which transcends all understanding, will guard
your hearts and your minds in Christ Jesus.*
PHILIPPIANS 4:6–7 NIV

*Don't worry about anything; instead, pray about everything.
Tell God what you need, and thank him for all he has done. Then you will
experience God's peace, which exceeds anything we can understand. His
peace will guard your hearts and minds as you live in Christ Jesus.*
PHILIPPIANS 4:6–7 NLT

TOPIC

Christian Life

INSIGHT

Paul encouraged the Philippian church, which was facing some
opposition, to trust in God and bring all their concerns to Him.

TIPS AND ENCOURAGEMENT

≡ As you memorize these verses, are you also putting them
into practice? This is a good verse to make a part of your
life. What actions does Paul tell the Philippians to put
into practice that can keep them from worrying? What are
the results they can expect?

REVIEW

Psalm 1:1–2
Luke 6:38
2 Timothy 3:16–17
Matthew 7:7–8

WEEK 42

BIBLE MEMORY VERSE

*And he said to them all, If any man will come
after me, let him deny himself, and take up his cross daily, and follow
me. For whosoever will save his life shall lose it: but whosoever will lose
his life for my sake, the same shall save it.*
LUKE 9:23–24 KJV

*Then he said to them all: "Whoever wants to be my disciple must deny
themselves and take up their cross daily and follow me. For whoever wants
to save their life will lose it, but whoever loses their life for me will save it."*
LUKE 9:23–24 NIV

*Then he said to the crowd, "If any of you wants to be my follower, you
must turn from your selfish ways, take up your cross daily,
and follow me. If you try to hang on to your life, you will lose it. But if
you give up your life for my sake, you will save it."*
LUKE 9:23–24 NLT

TOPIC

Seeking God

INSIGHT

Jesus warns that the Christian life is not a free ride. Just as our
salvation cost Him His life, a real faith is costly for us, too. But the
benefits of our small sacrifice now have eternal results.

TIPS AND ENCOURAGEMENT

≡ If you are having trouble remembering the chapter and verses of the texts you've memorized, spend some time connecting the two up in your mind. Focus on the reference before you say the verse, since the last part of your memorization may not easily stick in your mind. Remind yourself that you have not completed your memorization if you cannot tell where the verse is in scripture.

REVIEW

Galatians 2:20
Psalm 1:1–2
Luke 6:38
2 Timothy 3:16–17
Matthew 7:7–8
Philippians 4:6–7

WEEK 43

BIBLE MEMORY VERSE

Be sober, be vigilant; because your adversary the devil, as a roaring lion, walketh about, seeking whom he may devour: Whom resist stedfast in the faith, knowing that the same afflictions are accomplished in your brethren that are in the world.
1 PETER 5:8–9 KJV

Be alert and of sober mind. Your enemy the devil prowls around like a roaring lion looking for someone to devour. Resist him, standing firm in the faith, because you know that the family of believers throughout the world is undergoing the same kind of sufferings.
1 PETER 5:8–9 NIV

Stay alert! Watch out for your great enemy, the devil. He prowls around like a roaring lion, looking for someone to devour. Stand firm against him, and be strong in your faith. Remember that your Christian brothers and sisters all over the world are going through the same kind of suffering you are.
1 PETER 5:8–9 NLT

TOPIC

Christian Life

INSIGHT

Though the Christian life brings joy, it also has a serious side. The accuser, Satan, lies in wait to tempt frivolous believers. Peter calls God's people to be earnest in their belief and stand against opposition.

TIPS AND ENCOURAGEMENT

≡ No matter what trial you face, God knows about it. When God commands you to stand firm, He also provides you with the strength to do it, as you trust in Him. This applies to Bible memorization, too!

≡ Knowing you will face opposition, prepare for it by studying and memorizing God's Word. It will strengthen and encourage you and help you to respond to those who attack your faith. The more verses you have under your belt, the better prepared you will be.

REVIEW

2 Timothy 3:16–17
Matthew 7:7–8
Philippians 4:6–7
Luke 9:23–24

WEEK 44

BIBLE MEMORY VERSE

That if thou shalt confess with thy mouth the Lord Jesus, and shalt believe in thine heart that God hath raised him from the dead, thou shalt be saved. For with the heart man believeth unto righteousness; and with the mouth confession is made unto salvation.
ROMANS 10:9–10 KJV

*If you declare with your mouth, "Jesus is Lord," and believe in your
heart that God raised him from the dead, you will be saved.
For it is with your heart that you believe and are justified,
and it is with your mouth that you profess
your faith and are saved.*
ROMANS 10:9–10 NIV

*If you confess with your mouth that Jesus is Lord and believe
in your heart that God raised him from the dead, you will be saved.
For it is by believing in your heart that you are made
right with God, and it is by confessing with
your mouth that you are saved.*
ROMANS 10:9–10 NLT

TOPIC

Salvation

INSIGHT

God calls on Christians to share their faith so that all may hear of
His gracious love. To be a Christian, one cannot believe in anyone
but Christ. Being a Christian also takes a serious commitment and
trust in Him alone.

TIPS AND ENCOURAGEMENT

≡ Many people balk at this scriptural truth because they'd
   like to go with the flow and believe that heaven has no
   limitations. But this verse points out the critical part of
   belief in Christ: the truth that He is the only way to God.
   It is an important truth to be able to share with others.

≡ Do you avoid memorizing verses that are uncomfortable?
   Memorizing the "happy" verses of scripture may be
   encouraging to you and others, but if you do only that,
   you are avoiding the whole counsel of God. Don't miss
   out on all God wants you to know about Him and His
   salvation.

REVIEW

Matthew 7:7–8
Philippians 4:6–7
Luke 9:23–24
1 Peter 5:8–9

WEEK 45

BIBLE MEMORY VERSE

The LORD is my rock, and my fortress, and my deliverer; my God, my strength, in whom I will trust; my buckler, and the horn of my salvation, and my high tower. I will call upon the LORD, who is worthy to be praised: so shall I be saved from mine enemies.
PSALM 18:2–3 KJV

The LORD is my rock, my fortress and my deliverer; my God is my rock, in whom I take refuge, my shield and the horn of my salvation, my stronghold. I called to the LORD, who is worthy of praise, and I have been saved from my enemies.
PSALM 18:2–3 NIV

The LORD is my rock, my fortress, and my savior; my God is my rock, in whom I find protection. He is my shield, the power that saves me, and my place of safety. I called on the LORD, who is worthy of praise, and he saved me from my enemies.
PSALM 18:2–3 NLT

TOPIC

Our God

INSIGHT

David penned these words after God had rescued him from his enemies, including King Saul, who sought his life. If David could trust the Lord in such circumstances, how much more can we trust Him?

TIPS AND ENCOURAGEMENT

- Petra's song "I Will Call upon the Lord" may help you with verse 3, if you use the King James Version of the Bible for your memorization. If this tune is already in your head, you have the verse memorized!

- When you have memorized verse 3, you have also memorized 2 Samuel 22:4, since it is repeated there.

REVIEW

Philippians 4:6–7
Luke 9:23–24
1 Peter 5:8–9
Romans 10:9–10

WEEK 46

BIBLE MEMORY VERSE

Surely he hath borne our griefs, and carried our sorrows: yet we did esteem him stricken, smitten of God, and afflicted. But he was wounded for our transgressions, he was bruised for our iniquities: the chastisement of our peace was upon him; and with his stripes we are healed.
ISAIAH 53:4–5 KJV

Surely he took up our pain and bore our suffering, yet we considered him punished by God, stricken by him, and afflicted. But he was pierced for our transgressions, he was crushed for our iniquities; the punishment that brought us peace was on him, and by his wounds we are healed.
ISAIAH 53:4–5 NIV

*Yet it was our weaknesses he carried; it was our sorrows that weighed
him down. And we thought his troubles were a punishment from God,
a punishment for his own sins! But he was pierced for our rebellion,
crushed for our sins. He was beaten so we could be whole.
He was whipped so we could be healed.*
ISAIAH 53:4–5 NLT

TOPIC

Salvation

INSIGHT

Centuries before Jesus was born, the prophet Isaiah spoke these
words of Jesus, the Suffering Servant, who would die for our sins.

TIPS AND ENCOURAGEMENT

≡   Rather than giving up on a memorization passage
    because it seems "too long," break it up into two weeks of
    memorization. Better to keep up with a consistent pattern
    than to give up on your memorization plan. But you may
    also find that doing the whole passage is easier than you
    think. Read over the whole passage as you start your
    memorization, then begin memorizing as usual. You may
    find you have completed the whole passage by the end of
    the week.

≡   If you are a fan of Handel's oratorio *Messiah*, these words
    may be familiar to you. Let that help you along with your
    memorization.

REVIEW

Luke 9:23–24
1 Peter 5:8–9
Romans 10:9–10
Psalm 18:2–3

WEEK 47

BIBLE MEMORY VERSE

*And thou shalt love the Lord thy God with all thy heart,
and with all thy soul, and with all thy mind, and with all thy strength:
this is the first commandment. And the second is like, namely this,
Thou shalt love thy neighbour as thyself. There is none
other commandment greater than these.*
MARK 12:30–31 KJV

*"'Love the Lord your God with all your heart and with all
your soul and with all your mind and with all your strength.'
The second is this: 'Love your neighbor as yourself.'
There is no commandment greater than these."*
MARK 12:30–31 NIV

*"'And you must love the LORD your God with all your heart, all your
soul, all your mind, and all your strength.' The second is equally
important: 'Love your neighbor as yourself.'
No other commandment is greater than these."*
MARK 12:30–31 NLT

TOPIC

Christian Life

INSIGHT

Jewish law included many commandments on how to please
God, from rituals to guidelines for personal piety. When a scribe
asked Jesus which one was the most important, this was His
response.

TIPS AND ENCOURAGEMENT

≡ The focus of your memorization should be improving
your walk with the Lord by coming to know His
commandments. But knowing the words alone will be an
empty effort if your relationship with God isn't warm and
deep. How can this verse help you reach that goal?

187

REVIEW

1 Peter 5:8–9
Romans 10:9–10
Psalm 18:2–3
Isaiah 53:4–5

WEEK 48

BIBLE MEMORY VERSE

*Go ye therefore, and teach all nations, baptizing them in the name of the
Father, and of the Son, and of the Holy Ghost: Teaching them to observe
all things whatsoever I have commanded you: and, lo, I am with you
always, even unto the end of the world. Amen.*
MATTHEW 28:19–20 KJV

*"Therefore go and make disciples of all nations, baptizing them in the
name of the Father and of the Son and of the Holy Spirit, and teaching
them to obey everything I have commanded you. And surely I am with
you always, to the very end of the age."*
MATTHEW 28:19–20 NIV

*"Therefore, go and make disciples of all the nations, baptizing them in
the name of the Father and the Son and the Holy Spirit. Teach these new
disciples to obey all the commands I have given you. And be sure of this:
I am with you always, even to the end of the age."*
MATTHEW 28:19–20 NLT

TOPIC

Faith

INSIGHT

Known as the Great Commission, these verses, spoken by Jesus,
have inspired Christians throughout the ages to spread the Good
News of Jesus.

TIPS AND ENCOURAGEMENT

≡ God not only encourages us and tells us about Himself through scripture, He also commands us to take action concerning our beliefs. How is this a challenge to you? An encouragement?

REVIEW

Luke 9:23–24
1 Peter 5:8–9
Romans 10:9–10
Psalm 18:2–3
Isaiah 53:4–5
Mark 12:30–31

WEEK 49

BIBLE MEMORY VERSE

Therefore I say unto you, Take no thought for your life, what ye shall eat, or what ye shall drink; nor yet for your body, what ye shall put on. Is not the life more than meat, and the body than raiment? Behold the fowls of the air: for they sow not, neither do they reap, nor gather into barns; yet your heavenly Father feedeth them. Are ye not much better than they?
MATTHEW 6:25–26 KJV

"Therefore I tell you, do not worry about your life, what you will eat or drink; or about your body, what you will wear. Is not life more than food, and the body more than clothes? Look at the birds of the air; they do not sow or reap or store away in barns, and yet your heavenly Father feeds them. Are you not much more valuable than they?"
MATTHEW 6:25–26 NIV

"That is why I tell you not to worry about everyday life — whether you have enough food and drink, or enough clothes to wear. Isn't life more than food, and your body more than clothing? Look at the birds. They don't plant or harvest or store food in barns, for your heavenly Father feeds them. And aren't you far more valuable to him than they are?"
MATTHEW 6:25–26 NLT

TOPIC

Seeking God

INSIGHT

This comforting passage turns Christians away from concern about daily needs and toward trust of God. He knows our every need, and we can seek His kingdom without worrying that He will fail us.

TIPS AND ENCOURAGEMENT

≡ Begin to think about verses you'd like to memorize when you finish the *Bible Memory Plan*. You may begin with those in More Verses to Memorize, at the end of the book, but you will also need to create a plan that helps you memorize for the rest of your life. If you have a favorite devotional, such as *My Utmost for His Highest*, perhaps you will want to use the daily verses as fuel for your memorization. If your Bible study recommends verses, you may want to use them.

≡ To create a memorization plan, you could also copy down verses as you read your Bible or use other materials to study the Word. Write them on file cards and place them in a file card box, available at any stationery store, then use them as you need them. Just make certain you do not repeat the verses you already have memorized!

REVIEW

Psalm 18:2–3
Isaiah 53:4–5
Mark 12:30–31
Matthew 28:19–20

WEEK 50

BIBLE MEMORY VERSE

For God so loved the world, that he gave his only begotten Son, that whosoever believeth in him should not perish, but have everlasting life. For God sent not his Son into the world to condemn the world; but that the world through him might be saved. He that believeth on him is not condemned: but he that believeth not is condemned already, because he hath not believed in the name of the only begotten Son of God.
JOHN 3:16–18 KJV

"For God so loved the world that he gave his one and only Son, that whoever believes in him shall not perish but have eternal life. For God did not send his Son into the world to condemn the world, but to save the world through him. Whoever believes in him is not condemned, but whoever does not believe stands condemned already because they have not believed in the name of God's one and only Son."
JOHN 3:16–18 NIV

"For God loved the world so much that he gave his one and only Son, so that everyone who believes in him will not perish but have eternal life. God sent his Son into the world not to judge the world, but to save the world through him. There is no judgment against anyone who believes in him. But anyone who does not believe in him has already been judged for not believing in God's one and only Son."
JOHN 3:16–18 NLT

TOPIC

Salvation

INSIGHT

John 3:16 is probably the most familiar Bible verse. But how many people have memorized the verses that follow? By memorizing them, we complete our picture of the salvation God offers to those who will believe.

TIPS AND ENCOURAGEMENT

≡ Don't shrug off memorizing familiar verses because you feel you know them too well and it would be too easy. Instead, place them in context by memorizing some verses around them, too. You'll have a challenge and will be able to make effective use of the verse you already know.

REVIEW

Isaiah 53:4–5
Mark 12:30–31
Matthew 28:19–20
Matthew 6:25–26

WEEK 51

BIBLE MEMORY VERSE

But now the righteousness of God without the law is manifested, being witnessed by the law and the prophets; even the righteousness of God which is by faith of Jesus Christ unto all and upon all them that believe: for there is no difference: For all have sinned, and come short of the glory of God; being justified freely by his grace through the redemption that is in Christ Jesus.
ROMANS 3:21–24 KJV

But now apart from the law the righteousness of God has been made known, to which the Law and the Prophets testify. This righteousness is given through faith in Jesus Christ to all who believe. There is no difference between Jew and Gentile, for all have sinned and fall short of the glory of God, and are justified freely by his grace through the redemption that came by Christ Jesus.
ROMANS 3:21–24 NIV

But now God has shown us a way to be made right with him without keeping the requirements of the law, as was promised in the writings of Moses and the prophets long ago. We are made right with God by placing our faith in Jesus Christ. And this is true for everyone who

believes, no matter who we are. For everyone has sinned; we all fall short
of God's glorious standard. Yet God, with undeserved kindness, declares
that we are righteous. He did this through Christ Jesus when he freed us
from the penalty for our sins.
ROMANS 3:21–24 NLT

TOPIC

Salvation

INSIGHT

Nothing we can do will make us good enough to approach our
holy God. The apostle Paul knew this from personal experience,
since he had been a zealous Jew, rigorous in his observance of the
Law. Only faith in Jesus justifies us with the Lord.

TIPS AND ENCOURAGEMENT

≡ When you choose verses to memorize on your own, pick
some that are shorter and some that are longer. That way
you will be able to keep up with your memorization plan
even when your life is busy.

≡ Choose verses on different topics, so that you get a good
command of God's Word. Though you may want to
memorize one topic for an extended period of time, be
certain you don't become stuck in one area, or you'll be a
one-sided Christian in your Bible memorization.

≡ As you've moved through the book, the verses you've
memorized have gotten longer. Has memorization
become easier, or have you simply figured out the best
way to memorize? Either way, congratulations on your
accomplishment.

REVIEW

Mark 12:30–31
Matthew 28:19–20
Matthew 6:25–26
John 3:16–18

WEEK 52

BIBLE MEMORY VERSE

Wherefore seeing we also are compassed about with so great a cloud of witnesses, let us lay aside every weight, and the sin which doth so easily beset us, and let us run with patience the race that is set before us, looking unto Jesus the author and finisher of our faith; who for the joy that was set before him endured the cross, despising the shame, and is set down at the right hand of the throne of God.
HEBREWS 12:1–2 KJV

Therefore, since we are surrounded by such a great cloud of witnesses, let us throw off everything that hinders and the sin that so easily entangles. And let us run with perseverance the race marked out for us, fixing our eyes on Jesus, the pioneer and perfecter of faith. For the joy set before him he endured the cross, scorning its shame, and sat down at the right hand of the throne of God.
HEBREWS 12:1–2 NIV

Therefore, since we are surrounded by such a huge crowd of witnesses to the life of faith, let us strip off every weight that slows us down, especially the sin that so easily trips us up. And let us run with endurance the race God has set before us. We do this by keeping our eyes on Jesus, the champion who initiates and perfects our faith. Because of the joy awaiting him, he endured the cross, disregarding its shame. Now he is seated in the place of honor beside God's throne.
HEBREWS 12:1–2 NLT

TOPIC

Our God

INSIGHT

We do not run the faith race alone: Others have gone before us and have successfully completed the course. We can look to them for inspiration when the course becomes hard and our breathing labored. If we keep Jesus in our minds and hearts as we run, we will be victorious.

Tips and Encouragement

≡ If memorizing scripture becomes drudgery, you will not keep on doing it. Find ways to keep it fresh. Make it a part of your daily spiritual life and growth.

≡ During dry spiritual times, focus on verses that speak to your situation. Trust in God's ability to work in your life. Or work on verses that remind you how much God has done in your life.

≡ How has your memorization this year made a difference in your life? Have you seen how God has blessed you?

Review

Isaiah 53:4–5
Mark 12:30–31
Matthew 28:19–20
Matthew 6:25–26
John 3:16–18
Romans 3:21–24

More Verses to Memorize

You may memorize these in any order that pleases you. If you wish to memorize shorter passages, break down larger passages into single verses or a group of verses and memorize them for a number of weeks.

Psalm 23
Psalm 30:11–12
Psalm 32:1–2
Psalm 100
Psalm 121:3–8*
Proverbs 14:1
Proverbs 16:3
Matthew 6:27–30*
Matthew 6:33–34
John 1:3–5*
Romans 8:26–27*

Romans 8:29–30*
1 Corinthians 3:18–19
Ephesians 6:12–13*
Philippians 3:12–14
Philippians 4:8*
Colossians 1:15–20
Hebrews 11:1–3
1 Peter 1:14–15
1 Peter 1:23
1 John 2:15–17

*A continuation of verses already memorized.

HOW DID WE GET the BIBLE?

Tracy Macon Sumner

Contents

Preface

If you're a Bible-believing Christian, you no doubt know that the Bible is no ordinary book. It is the very Word of God Himself, which He spoke and then had recorded, protected, preserved, and compiled for the benefit of His people. As such, you can know that every word of the Bible is truth; that you can count on it as your guide for your life of faith; and that God will make good on every promise recorded in its pages.

But how did He do it? How did God inspire people and arrange events so that the words He spoke through His Holy Spirit were accurately recorded and compiled, then preserved and passed down from generation to generation throughout the centuries?

The word *amazing* doesn't begin to describe the process God used to give us His written Word. From the time the actual writing began, some thirty-five centuries ago, until now, God has miraculously used imperfect people to give the world the one perfect book. God gave people—people He specifically chose to do the work of bringing forth the books of the Bible—the words He wanted them to write, then set in motion the events that led to the compilation and translation of the sixty-six books we have in the Bible today.

Though a book that lays out all the details of how we got the Bible could easily run to thousands of pages and include hundreds of names, dates, and events, this little book gives the reader a briefer, more concise overview of the people God used and the events He ordained to give us the most important book ever written.

This book will first give you snapshot accounts of the men (and possibly a woman or two) that God used to record His written Word. From there, it will tell you how He protected and preserved that written Word, moved people to compile the books we have in our Bible today, and made provision for us to have available a printed copy of that Word in our own language.

Most Christians have at least a basic grasp of the message of salvation that is presented throughout the Bible. Most also have some knowledge of the stories contained in its pages: from the story of Adam and Eve, to the account of Israel's exodus from Egypt, to the eyewitness testimonies of those who saw the deeds and heard the acts of Jesus Christ during His earthly ministry, to the men Jesus chose to spread His gospel message throughout the world. Comparatively few, however, understand how the stories, promises, warnings, and encouragements contained in the Bible came to be recorded for us to read today.

As you read through this book—even if you have a good grasp of the actual contents of the Bible—you may find yourself saying, "I hadn't thought of that before!" But God did! Looking forward from eternity past, He knew His people would need the Bible as their handbook for a life of faith, and He did everything necessary to make sure we, as well as believers before us and after us, could have access to everything He has to say about a victorious, growing life of faith in Him.

1

God's Transmitters

The People Who
Wrote the Bible

Take a look for a minute at your personal Bible. Have you ever wondered who was responsible for recording all the wonderful stories, promises, commands, and words of encouragement found in every book and on every page? Did God just drop them into someone's hand and say, "There's your Bible!"? Or did a bunch of people who lived long ago just sit around thinking about God and the things He had said and done and then just start writing?

The real story of how we got the books of the Bible is actually a lot more complex—and fascinating—than that. And it's also a lot more inspiring, for it demonstrates how God used ordinary, fallible people—people just like us today—to give us His infallible written Word. More on those people later, but first let's take a look at *how* God used these people to do what no one could have done on his or her own.

More than forty men (and possibly a few women) wrote the books we have in our Bible today. They came from a wide variety of backgrounds and vocations. In the Old Testament, for example, Moses was a shepherd, David a warrior and king, Ezra a priest, Isaiah (and other writers of the Bible's "prophetic" books) a prophet of God, and Amos a fig farmer. The same kind of variety can be found among the New Testament writers. Matthew was a tax collector, Peter and John were fishermen, Luke was a physician and historian, and the apostle Paul was a tent maker and a devout Jewish religious leader.

Because we are imperfect people who live with other imperfect people, we know how hard it is to get three people—never mind more than forty—to agree on anything, let alone present consistent communication on a given subject. But the Bible never strays from its message, never contradicts itself, and always presents God's plan of redemption for humankind with perfect consistency.

But how did such a diverse group of writers—most of whom never met one another—pull that off?

The answer lies in the word *inspiration*.

When God Spoke, These People Listened—and Wrote!

As the apostle Paul declares, "All Scripture is given by inspiration of God" (2 Timothy 3:16). Most of us have a pretty good idea what it means to be inspired to do, say, or write something. Most every artist, poet, musician, or novelist can point to his or her own work and tell you exactly what inspired him or her to do it. Emotions such as love, anger, hatred, or grief have inspired artistic types throughout the centuries.

But in the context of scripture, the word *inspiration* means more than receiving an idea or an inkling of what to say or write. It means more than seeing a need for a particular message and writing it down. It means that God, through His Holy Spirit, spoke through a person and gave him or her His very own words to record. In short, the people who wrote the books of the Bible were instruments that God miraculously used—pencils in His hand, as someone once put it—to give us His written Word, the Bible.

That is precisely why some translations of the Bible render 2 Timothy 3:16 more literally, telling us that all scripture is "God-breathed," which means that God Himself spoke the words you read in the pages of your Bible today.

The apostle Peter, who was with Jesus during His earthly ministry, expounds on the truth that the Bible is the inspired Word of God when he writes, "No prophecy of Scripture is of any private interpretation, for prophecy never came by the will of man, but holy men of God spoke as they were moved by the Holy Spirit" (2 Peter 1:20–21).

Although the Bible was written by dozens of fallible human individuals from greatly diverse walks of life, it has one ultimate Author, and that's God Himself. The Bible is both the history of God's interactions with His people and the rest of the world, and His instruction manual for living a life that pleases Him—also known as a life of faith.

That's why you can count on the Bible as your ultimate source for everything you need to know to live a life of true faith and obedience to the author and finisher of that faith (see Hebrews 12:2).

How It All Started—the Old Testament

The Old Testament traces the story of how humankind got its start; how sin corrupted a once-perfect creation; and how God set in motion the events, and prepared the people He used, to send Jesus Christ to redeem a fallen, sinful world.

The Old Testament is chock-full of some of the most familiar characters and stories in the Bible (Adam and Eve in the Garden of Eden, Noah and his ark, Israel's exodus from Egypt, and Jonah's three days in the belly of a giant sea creature—just to name a few), but more importantly, it demonstrates the power and care of a God who was constantly busy working (both up front and behind the scenes) to make sure His plan for redemption was brought to completion.

Here are the people God used to record the events and promises found in the Old Testament:

Moses—Though the book of Genesis doesn't name an author, many centuries of tradition hold that it was written by Moses, God's chosen man to lead the people of Israel out of Egyptian captivity. Moses is also credited with writing Exodus (see Exodus 17:14, 24:4–7, 34:27), Leviticus, Deuteronomy, and Numbers. It has also been suggested that Moses recorded the book of Job, which is widely believed to be the oldest book in the Bible. He also wrote one of the Psalms.

Joshua—The book of Joshua also doesn't specifically identify its author, but Jewish tradition and most modernday Bible scholars hold that Joshua, Moses' successor as leader of Israel and the man who led the people of Israel into the Promised Land, recorded *most* of the book himself (see Joshua 24:26). The latter part of the book was obviously written after his death.

Samuel—Tradition holds that the prophet Samuel, the last of the judges who presided over the nation of Israel, authored the book of Judges. It is also possible, but not certain, that he wrote the book of Ruth and parts of 1 and 2 Samuel.

Ezra and Nehemiah—According to Jewish tradition, Ezra, who led a second wave of exiles back to Judah from the Babylonian Captivity (around 605–530 BC), wrote parts of the book that bears his name (though it is apparent from the tone of the book that he didn't write all of it), and also compiled and edited 1 and 2 Chronicles. Ezra or Nehemiah may have authored the book of Nehemiah, which is widely thought to be Nehemiah's autobiography.

The Book of Esther—Though this book doesn't name its author, the most popular and lasting tradition says that Mordecai, a major character in the story, recorded the book, which gives the account of heroism in the face of a threatened genocide against the Hebrew people. Another possible author is Nehemiah.

The Book of Job—As mentioned earlier, Moses may have written the book of Job, which is the account of the suffering of a righteous man who had done nothing to deserve it. Other possible authors are King Solomon or Job himself.

Solomon—Israel's third monarch, the son of King David, is widely credited with writing the first twenty-nine chapters of Proverbs (Agur wrote Proverbs 30, and Lemuel wrote Proverbs 31), as well as Ecclesiastes and the Song of Solomon. His writings contain excellent examples of godly wisdom, as well as encouragements to remain in the faith.

Isaiah—Isaiah, the son of Amoz, who ministered to the people of Judah through the reigns of four different kings, recorded his own book of prophecies, which is the Old Testament book most often quoted in the New Testament. Isaiah prophesied from the time of King Uzziah (around 740 BC) to the time of King Hezekiah (around 681 BC). Isaiah's message is one of God's intolerance of sin, of judgment for that sin, and of hope, for the Messiah is coming to provide atonement for the sin of humankind.

Jeremiah—The "weeping prophet," so called because of the mournful tone of his prophecies concerning the coming destruction of Jerusalem, penned the book of prophecies that bears his name and the companion book of Lamentations. He is also believed, according to Jewish tradition, and according to many biblical scholars, to have recorded 1 Kings and 2 Kings. Jeremiah's prophecies cover the dark period of time in Judah's history from the thirteenth year of the reign of King Josiah (627 BC) until several years after the Babylonian invasion (586 BC), which he foretold.

Ezekiel—The prophet and priest Ezekiel ministered to the people of Judah just before and during the Babylonian Captivity, recording his prophecies in the book that bears his name. Ezekiel's prophetic book is seen as a companion piece to that of Jeremiah, but Ezekiel focuses more on God's message of restoration for His people once they repent of their sin.

Daniel—Daniel, who is never referred to as a prophet in his book, recorded his life experiences and prophecies, which cover a time during and shortly after the Babylonian Captivity. Daniel's prophecies foretold the coming of several key historic figures, such as Alexander the Great, Cleopatra, and most importantly, Jesus Christ. They also foretell the coming of the Antichrist, as well as the second coming of Jesus Christ at the end of days.

The "Minor" Prophets—Don't let the term "minor prophet" fool you. These twelve Old Testament prophets recorded books containing shorter (but still important) "God-breathed" prophecies for different times and different groups throughout the history of Israel:

- **Hosea**—Hosea was a prophet of God who lived and served in Israel around the time of the reigns of kings Uzziah, Jotham, Ahaz, and Hezekiah of Judah, and Jeroboam of Israel. God commanded Hosea to marry a prostitute named Gomer, as an illustration of both the waywardness of God's people and of His never-ending love for them and willingness to do what it took to "win" them back.

- **Joel**—This prophet, identified as "the son of Pethuel" (Joel 1:1), was a well-educated man who knew the words of the earlier prophets, and who used an invasion of locusts (figurative or literal) on Judah to illustrate a coming judgment, specifically against Jerusalem, if the people didn't awaken from their spiritual lethargy. The historic context of Joel's prophecy isn't certain, but it is believed he wrote during the reign of King Joash (835–796 BC).

- **Amos**—This farmer-turned-prophet from the town of Tekoa in Judah prophesied to Israel and Judah, as well as surrounding nations, during the reign of King Uzziah of Judah and King Jeroboam II of Israel. This was a time of prosperity in Israel, but also a time of deep spiritual malaise. Amos's prophecies pronounce judgment for that malaise, but they also express hope for those who wholeheartedly turn back to God.

- **Obadiah**—Obadiah wrote his prophecy—nineteen verses in a single chapter, the shortest book in the Old Testament—which foretells the destruction of Edom for its opposition to the nation of Israel (around 840 BC). Nothing is known of Obadiah's personal history.

- **Jonah**—If the extent of your knowledge of the Bible is limited to what you heard in Sunday school as a child, you know that Jonah was the wayward prophet who ran from God and ended up spending three days in the belly of a giant sea creature. Jonah lived and served around the time of the reign of King Jeroboam II (around 760 BC). After God restored him, Jonah preached to the city of Nineveh, which repented and was spared destruction.

- **Micah**—A native of southern Judah, Micah prophesied during the reigns of kings Jotham, Ahaz, and Hezekiah (750–686 BC). His prophecies were against the princes and people of Judah for their abusive treatment of the poor.

- **Nahum**—Nahum prophesied in the years around 660 BC, and his prophecies proclaim the fall of Nineveh, the same city that one hundred years earlier had repented at the preaching of Jonah and was spared. All that is known of Nahum's personal life is that he was born in a place called Elkosh (see Nahum 1:1).

- **Habakkuk**—The rebellious, hard-hearted nation of Judah was about to be invaded by the Babylonians. God told Habakkuk that this judgment was coming.

Though Habakkuk didn't understand why God would use such evil people to judge His own people, he acknowledged that God knew what He was doing—as well as the best way to do it.

- **Zephaniah**—A contemporary of Jeremiah's and the son of a man named Cushi (see Zephaniah 1:1), Zephaniah wrote of a coming judgment on the people of Israel, but he also wrote of God's promises of eventual restoration and salvation for His people.

- **Haggai**—The Jews had returned to Judah from the Babylonian Exile, and God had made their top priority the construction of a new temple to replace the old one, which the Babylonians destroyed seventy years earlier. Haggai's prophecies chided the people for not finishing what they had started sixteen years earlier, upon their return to their homeland, and commanded them to again get busy with the work.

- **Zechariah**—Like Haggai, Zechariah, who identifies himself as "the son of Berechiah" (Zechariah 1:1), focuses his writing on the need to complete the construction of the new temple in Jerusalem. The first eight chapters focus on the command to complete the project, the final six on the promises of blessing for doing so.

- **Malachi**—The Old Testament closes with the writings of the prophet Malachi, who was a contemporary of Nehemiah's. Malachi's prophecies chided the people of Judah for falling into the same kind of sins that had led to the destruction of Jerusalem and the seven decades of captivity in Babylon.

Some "New Covenant" Writing

The Bible as a whole is the story of God's plan for the redemption of humankind. The Old Testament is more or less the story of His "laying the groundwork" for bringing salvation to the world, and the New Testament tells the story of how God sent His Son, Jesus Christ, into the world to bring the news and do the work of that salvation (see John 3:16), and then what that gift means to individual believers.

Christianity Gets Its Start

If you want to learn all the Bible has to say about the life of Jesus Christ, and about the beginning of the Christian faith following Christ's death and resurrection, you'll find it in the first five books of the New Testament—the four Gospels and the book of Acts (also called the Acts of the Apostles).

Now take a moment to get to know some of the New Testament writers:

Matthew—Talk about a transformation! Here's a man who was part of the most hated class of people in first-century Israel—tax collectors for the Roman government, whom the Jewish people saw as the worst of sinners—but who heard and obeyed Jesus' call to follow Him (see Matthew 9:9; Luke 5:27–28) and later wrote the Gospel intended specifically for the first wave of Jewish believers.

Mark—Most scholars believe that the author of the Gospel of Mark was a young man named John Mark, who is mentioned by name in the book of Acts as a traveling companion of the apostles Paul and Barnabas (see Acts 12:25). It is also widely believed that the young man who fled the scene of Jesus' arrest in the Garden of Gethsemane naked (see Mark 14:51–52) was also John Mark.

Luke—Luke, a first-century historian, physician, and missionary who wrote the Gospel bearing his name, as well as the book of Acts, is unique among the writers of biblical books in that he is the only Gentile (non-Jew) to write a book of the Bible. It is believed that Luke accompanied Paul in his later missionary journeys, because he changes the narrative in Acts to include himself (see Acts 16:11). Luke's skill as a writer and historian are amply demonstrated in the book of Acts, as well as in his Gospel, which is the most detailed and historical of the four.

John—The apostle who refers to himself as the disciple "whom Jesus loved" (John 13:23) was a fisherman-turned-disciple who wrote the Gospel of John, as well as the three epistles bearing his name (1, 2, and 3 John) and the book of Revelation. Jesus referred to John and his brother James, the sons of a fisherman named Zebedee (see Matthew 4:21), as *Boanerges*, which means "Sons of Thunder" (Mark 3:17), the meaning of which isn't explained.

The Epistles: Words to Live By!

If you're like most people, when you've finished reading the Gospels and the book of Acts, you will likely ask how you can practically apply what you've just read in your own walk of faith. You'll find answers in the next twenty-one books of the New Testament, which will give you practical commandments, guidelines, and promises for living the Christian life.

These "epistles"—or letters—were written to various individuals, churches, and groups of believers to encourage, challenge, and instruct them in the specifics of an individual's life of faith in Christ and of the basics of life within the church body.

There are five known writers of the New Testament epistles, including the apostle John. Here is the lowdown on the others:

Paul—Humanly speaking, if you were going to appoint someone as the "apostle to the Gentiles" (Romans 11:13; Ephesians 3:8) and as the human author of most of the books of the New Testament, it wouldn't be this guy. Paul (he was called Saul before his conversion) was a devout Jewish religious leader in first-century Jerusalem who spent a lot of his time persecuting the fledgling church (see 1 Timothy 1:13). But after a spectacular conversion experience on the road to Damascus (he was on his way to that city to cause more trouble for the church there), Paul spent the remainder of his life faithfully and passionately following God's call to preach the gospel of Christ to the non-Jewish world. He planted new churches in various cities around the region, and wrote letters to those churches that would later become an important part of the New Testament. Paul is known with certainty to have written the epistles of Romans, 1 and 2 Corinthians, Galatians, Ephesians, Philippians, Colossians, 1 and 2 Thessalonians, 1 and 2 Timothy, Titus, and Philemon. Some scholars believe he also wrote the epistle to the Hebrews, but differences in tone and style cast serious doubt on his authorship of that letter.

James—The New Testament mentions several men named James, but most scholars agree that the author of the epistle of James is "the Lord's brother" (Galatians 1:19; see also Mark 6:3), the son of Mary and Joseph.

Peter—Of the original twelve men Jesus called to be His apostles (see Matthew 4:18–20; Mark 1:16–18; Luke 5:1–11), none played a larger role in establishing the early church than Peter, the simple fisherman from the Sea of Galilee coastal town of Bethsaida, who received and followed Jesus' call to be His apostle to the Jews; who preached with power following Jesus' return to heaven (Acts 2:14–39); and who wrote the two epistles that bear his name. He was the brother of Andrew, another of the twelve apostles and the one who first introduced Peter to Jesus (John 1:40–42).

Jude—The authorship of the epistle of Jude is not certain, but Jude (or Judas) identifies himself as the brother of James (Jude 1). Though Jude doesn't identify himself as Jesus' earthly half brother, it is likely he was referring to Jesus' half brother James as his own brother.

So Why *These* Books by *These* People?

All of the writings that make up what we know as the Old Testament were completed by around 500 BC, and all the books that make up the New Testament we have today were finished by the end of the first century AD.

But what some Christians don't know is that the books included in our Bible weren't the only ones written concerning the history of the Jewish people, concerning the life of Jesus Christ, or concerning the life of faith in Christ. That leaves several questions unanswered for the average Bible reader. For example, how do we know that the Bible we have today says the same things the writers wrote thousands of years ago? And why were the books we have in the Bible now included, while others were left out?

For the answers to these allimportant questions, read chapter 2, which tells the story of how the truth of God's written Word has been preserved throughout the centuries. Then move on to chapter 3, which will tell you how we got what is called the "canon" of scripture.

2
Keeping the Bible
"On Message"
How God Has Preserved
His Written Word

Just about any Bible-believing Christian who has had a chance to talk to a skeptic about God's written Word has probably heard objections to the accuracy of the scriptures as we have them today. "How can you say the Bible is accurate?" the doubter protests. "The first books in the Bible were written thousands of years ago, so how is it possible that they say the same thing they did when they were written?"

A good question indeed, and one for which God has provided the answer.

Speaking through the prophet Isaiah, God told His people, "The grass withers, the flower fades, but the word of our God stands forever" (Isaiah 40:8). Jesus echoed the message behind those words when He told His disciples, "Heaven and earth will pass away, but My words will by no means pass away" (Matthew 24:35).

Obviously, God is passionately committed to doing whatever it takes to preserve His primary form of communication to His people, His written Word. And just as He used fallible men—

men He called and equipped—to give humankind His words, He later used fallible men to preserve and care for His Word.

Caretakers of God's Written Word

If you have even the most basic understanding of how God does things, you know that more often than not, He uses people to do things He could just as easily—and most of the time more effectively—do Himself. That includes the task of preserving and protecting His written Word and perpetuating it from generation to generation.

After all, the Bible tells us, that was God's purpose for choosing the people of Israel.

In his letter to the Romans, the apostle Paul writes, "What advantage then has the Jew, or what is the profit of circumcision? Much in every way! Chiefly because to them were committed the oracles of God" (Romans 3:1–2). In other words, God granted the people of Israel—His chosen people, according to scripture—many privileges, but He also entrusted them with the high and holy purpose of taking care of scripture and passing it on to future generations.

This was certainly an awesome and solemn task, a fact reflected in God's command to Moses: "You shall not add to the word which I command you, nor take from it, that you may keep the commandments of the LORD your God which I command you" (Deuteronomy 4:2). In other words, those who were entrusted with caring for the Word of God had to do so with great care, making certain that every one of His commands and promises was preserved perfectly.

Moses and the Levites

The first man charged with accurately recording the words of God was Moses, the man God chose to lead the people of Israel out of Egyptian captivity and slavery. Moses had a lot on his plate in those days. In addition to receiving and carrying out God's instructions for leading the Israelites (an awesome task for which God provided him help), Moses also had to write down what God said and everything that happened to him during those years (see Deuteronomy 31:24).

As Moses' death drew near, he entrusted the care and keeping of the Book of the Law (the first five books in the Bible) to the Levites, whose job it was to assist the priests of Israel. That included reading the books to the people of Israel every seven years (see Deuteronomy 31:9–13). Once Moses had completed his writing, he "commanded the Levites, who bore the ark of the covenant of the LORD, saying: 'Take this Book of the Law, and put it beside the ark of the covenant of the LORD your God' " (Deuteronomy 31:25–26).

From that time forward, as the Israelites took possession of the Promised Land, the Levites zealously carried out Moses' command to safeguard the scriptures. Eventually, however, that job fell into the hands of another group of men.

A Job Fit for a King

Though God had intended that He Himself would be king over the nation of Israel, He knew that the people would soon turn away from Him and ask to be given a human king, just like the nations around them (see Deuteronomy 17:14–15; 1 Samuel 8:1–9). Though it was not part of God's plan that a human king should rule Israel, He still lovingly made provision for the preservation of His written Word during the monarchy.

When God gave Moses the Book of the Law and commanded him to record everything He had said, He included instructions that the kings of Israel were to follow regarding the books: "Also it shall be, when he sits on the throne of his kingdom, that he shall write for himself a copy of this law in a book, from the one before the priests, the Levites. And it shall be with him, and he shall read it all the days of his life, that he may learn to fear the LORD his God and be careful to observe all the words of this law and these statutes" (Deuteronomy 17:18–19).

God was so committed to preserving His law, and so committed to making sure the kings of Israel knew and obeyed it, that He commanded each man who would later serve as king—Saul, David, Solomon, and so on—to make a copy of it for himself, using the books the Levites had preserved, and then carefully read and obey it for the rest of his life.

Again, however, the work of preserving the Book of the Law was passed on to another group of men.

A New Era of Bible Preservation

In 586 BC the Babylonians, under the command of King Nebuchadnezzar, sacked Jerusalem, looted and destroyed the holy temple, and took many of the people living there away from their home to Babylon, where they stayed for the next seventy years. This part of Israel's history is called the Babylonian Captivity.

Up until the day the Babylonians attacked Jerusalem, the Israelites still kept a copy of the Book of the Law inside the ark of the covenant, which was stored inside the temple. And though the temple itself was leveled by the Babylonians, the temple scriptures were preserved.

During the Babylonian Captivity, certain Levites began copying the scriptures and distributing them to the other Israelites living in Babylon. These Levites came to be known as *scribes*, and they gained distinction among the people for their unsurpassed knowledge of the scriptures, as well as their accuracy in copying them.

The scribes followed a painstaking process, which had been developed over time since the beginning of the monarchy in Israel, for faithfully reproducing copies of the books of the Law. This was many centuries before the development of any kind of printing technology, so they had to do their work by hand. That they did, while following a detailed, meticulous set of rules and regulations, all of which ensured that the job was done with complete accuracy.

Following a Process

The Jewish scribes knew they weren't handling just any set of writings. These were the words of God Himself they were copying, and they approached their work with the diligence and passion due such an important calling. They also held fast to the rules for the transcribing, which is recorded in the Talmud, an ancient record of discussions pertaining to Jewish law, ethics, customs, and history.

Here is a quick overview of those rules:

- The scribe was required to prepare a parchment and dedicate it to the Lord before he began his work. The parchments would be clean, using the skins of only clean animals, both for writing on and binding the manuscripts.
- Each column on the parchment could include no fewer than forty-eight lines, and no more than sixty lines. Letters and words alike had to be spaced at a certain distance, and no word could touch another. This helped avoid confusion in reading as well as errors in future copying.
- The ink used in the process was always black and of a special mixture used only for copying scripture.
- Even when the scribe had memorized a passage of scripture by heart, he was not allowed to write it down from memory. He was still required to copy from an authentic copy of scripture; and as he wrote, he had to pronounce every word aloud.
- Every time the scribe wrote the Hebrew word for the

name of God, he was required to wipe his pen clean and wash his entire body. This was in reverence for God and for His Word.

- After the copying was completed, the scroll was to be examined and checked for accuracy within thirty days. If the scribe made even one error, the entire sheet on which the mistake was made was destroyed. If mistakes were found on three separate pages, the entire manuscript was condemned.

- The scribe counted not just every word and paragraph in the manuscript, but every letter. Each paragraph, word, and letter had to correspond perfectly to the original.

Once the process of copying a manuscript was completed, the new copy could be stored only in sacred places, such as in a synagogue. No parchment containing the name of God could be destroyed, so when a copy became worn out and illegible in time, it was stored or buried in a *genizah*, which is a Hebrew word meaning a "hiding place," which was usually located in a synagogue or Jewish cemetery. This is why no original Old Testament manuscripts survive today.

This detailed and exacting process of copying and recopying the Hebrew scriptures in ancient times led to copies of the Old Testament that held incredibly true to their original words and intent. Some estimates hold that copies of the Old Testament text used in translating the Bible into English (see chapters 4 and 6) were 99.9 percent true to the original—with the only deviations being in updated spelling and punctuation.

Preserving the Word in the Christian Era

The Jewish scribes continued their work up to and after the time of Jesus' earthly ministry. That work continued even after the Roman destruction of Jerusalem in AD 70.

Eventually, the Masoretes, a line of Jewish scribes and scholars, took over the work of preserving the scriptures. Working between the sixth and eleventh centuries, these men used intricate number systems in their work and produced what is called the Masoretic Text, a highly accurate copy of the Old Testament text, which was the basis of most modern Bible translations.

While the work the scribes and Masoretes performed ensured that the Old Testament texts were preserved to perfection, God used other means to preserve the books of the New Testament.

New Testament Preservation

Bible skeptics often claim that the New Testament was written so long after the events depicted in the Gospels and the book of Acts that there is no way they can be considered reliable. They further hold that the content of all New Testament books has been copied and recopied so many times—by hand, no less—that the content has become degraded to the point where we can't know for certain exactly what the New Testament writers originally recorded.

The facts, however, don't support that kind of skepticism. On the contrary, they demonstrate the blessed truth that God worked through men to preserve not only the Old Testament, but the New Testament as well.

As of today, thousands—estimates range between four thousand and six thousand—of handwritten copies of the Greek New Testament have been discovered, as well as thousands more in other languages. Some of these manuscripts are complete Bibles, and others are complete books or pages. The oldest of the fragments—many of which are in museums around the world, including many in Europe and North America—date back as far as AD 130, with many others dated between the second and sixteenth centuries.

There is a wealth of ancient New Testament manuscripts and fragments available today, but the all-important question of our time is this: How close are they in content to our modern-day Bibles? Obviously, language has changed greatly over the past two thousand years, but has the actual content of the New Testament been changed in any significant way?

Experts who have studied the ancient New Testament manuscripts tell us that there are tens of thousands of variants found between them—and, of course, between those manuscripts and the New Testament we have today. However, the vast majority of those variations are relatively insignificant changes, such as misspellings, updated spellings, syntax, and other minor variants that have no effect on the actual content. Of the remaining variations, only five have been found to cast any doubt at all on the accuracy of the text. (If you carefully examine your own Bible, you'll probably find footnotes regarding five "questionable" passages: Mark 16:9–20; Luke 22:20, 43–44, 23:34; and John 7:53–8:11.)

Furthermore, the early church fathers—well-known Christian leaders from the second and third centuries of the Christian era—quoted the New Testament extensively in their writings, so extensively that, according to some scholars, all but eleven New Testament verses appear somewhere in their writings. In other words, it is nearly possible to reconstruct the *entire* New Testament from the church fathers' writings alone!

The bottom line, most Bible scholars tell us, is that most translations today contain essentially the same content as the first-century originals. In other words, the New Testament we have today is the same one written nearly two thousand years ago.

3
Why *These* Books?
The Compilation of the
Canon of Scripture

Writing to a young pastor named Timothy, the apostle Paul makes an important statement: "*All* Scripture is given by inspiration of God, and is profitable for doctrine, for reproof, for correction, for instruction in righteousness, that the man of God may be complete, thoroughly equipped for every good work" (2 Timothy 3:16–17, italics added).

This passage points out two very important facts about the Word of God. First, that God has "inspired" *all* scripture. In chapter one you read that the word *inspired* as it is used in this verse means that God, through the Holy Spirit, spoke His own words through the human writers of scripture.

Second, Paul communicated to Timothy that he, as well as every other believer past and present, could depend on the words of scripture as being the promises and warnings, the instructions and guidelines, that God has given to show believers how to live a growing, victorious life of faith.

But how can we know for certain that every word of every book in the Bible is indeed "inspired" and therefore "profitable for doctrine, reproof, for correction, for instruction in righteousness"?

At the time the canon of scripture—meaning the list of books considered "inspired" and authoritative, the books that met God's perfect standard—was established, there were many, many letters and "Gospels" making their way around what was then the Christian world. But nowhere in the Bible does God tell us specifically which books He intended to be part of His written Word.

So how do we know that the books of our Bible are the right ones? The answer lies in the great care God put into making sure all the words He inspired the biblical writers to record were kept in the blessed book He has prepared and given us.

That work, of course, began with the Old Testament.

The Hebrew Canon
of Scripture

The Hebrew scriptures—also known as the Old Testament—were written from the time period from about 1400 BC through around 400 BC, when the prophet Malachi recorded his book. All of these books were written in Hebrew and passed down from generation to generation of Jewish people, who from the time of their writing accepted them as the authentic, inspired Word of God.

Between 400 BC and the birth of Christ, several other books—known as the Apocrypha (see sidebar)—made their way into Jewish popular culture. But while the vast majority of Jews didn't accept these books as scripture, most valued these works as good literary sources of history and some spiritual insight.

By the time of Jesus' birth, the canon of Hebrew scripture was pretty much decided. The Jews recognized that Moses, the prophets, and other writers were God's messengers and therefore accepted their work as the inspired Word of God. About AD 90, Jewish elders met at the council at Jamnia (in Judea, near the Mediterranean coast) and affirmed the Hebrew canon, at the same time rejecting the books of the Apocrypha as scripture.

Around AD 95, Flavius Josephus, a Jewish historian and priest, recognized the Hebrew canon as the books now included in the Old Testament. (Like the council at Jamnia, he listed just twenty-two books, not thirty-nine, but that can be accounted for by the way books were kept in ancient times.)

By the mid-third century, the church was in almost complete agreement about the Hebrew canon of scripture—which is underscored by the fact that nowhere in the New Testament is any book outside the accepted Hebrew canon quoted, whereas the Old Testament is quoted extensively. There was, however, some debate about the books of the Apocrypha, which to this day are still included in some Roman Catholic Bibles but are not considered part of the canon in Protestant circles.

Even after the books of the Hebrew canon were completed, God was far from finished communicating with His people—and far from finished overseeing the complete list of books He wanted in His Bible.

Many Were Written, but Few Were Chosen

By the end of the first century of the Christian era, every book of what would later be known as the New Testament was completed. At least eight different people (depending on who wrote Hebrews) received the God-given words they recorded for the various churches and individuals to whom they ministered.

But the evidence points out that these people also produced other writings, most of which have long since been lost. For example, 1 Corinthians 5:9 tells us that the apostle Paul had written an earlier letter to the Corinthian church. Knowing that, it's hard to imagine that Paul, Peter, James, Matthew, and other New Testament writers didn't produce other writings not now included in the New Testament.

In addition to the "extra-biblical" writings of the apostles, there were scores of documents written during the first few centuries of Christianity that weren't included in the canon of scripture—some because they were written too late to be included, and others whose content was highly questionable, or patently heretical, or whose authorship was suspect.

Finally, there were writings by the earliest of the church leaders, including Clement (died around AD 99), the first-century bishop of Rome, who wrote a letter to the church at Corinth around AD 95. Ignatius (around AD 35 to around 110), a bishop of Antioch in Syria, also sent letters to the Ephesian, Magnasian, Trallian, Roman, Philadelphian, and Smyrnan churches, as well as to Polycarp (around AD 70 to around 155), the Greek bishop of Smyrna.

What to Leave in, What to Leave Out

Though the canon of scripture wasn't officially recognized—at least by any human institution—until the fourth century AD, the early church recognized the authenticity of certain letters and books far earlier than that. During the first few centuries of Christianity, the church had several criteria for recognizing a writing as being truly inspired. Some of these criteria applied to the writers themselves (for example, was the writer recognized as a true prophet of God whose authority was confirmed by the presence of miracles?), and some applied to the writing itself (for example, does the writing tell the absolute truth about God, and without contradiction or deceit?). All of the books the church used and recognized as inspired during those early years met those criteria.

The process of canonizing the New Testament books began during the times of the apostles, some of whom recognized one another's writings as inspired, and therefore scriptural. For example, the apostle Paul quoted the writings of Luke and referred to them as being scripture on a par with the Old Testament (see

1 Timothy 5:18; compare with Luke 10:7). Peter acknowledged that Paul's writings were truly inspired, even likening them to "the rest of the Scriptures" (2 Peter 3:16).

Also, the early believers of that time recognized the writings of the New Testament apostles and others as scripture. These early Christians immediately recognized the apostles as men divinely appointed and gifted to communicate God's Word to the world around them. That is why the Bible tells us that they "welcomed it not as the word of men, but as it is in truth, the word of God, which also effectively works in you who believe" (1 Thessalonians 2:13), and why they obeyed the apostles' instructions to spread their writings to believers throughout the known world (see Colossians 4:16; 1 Thessalonians 5:27).

The process of acknowledging the canon of New Testament scripture continued during the time of the early church fathers—between the first and third centuries AD Clement, in his writings to various churches, made mention of at least eight books that are included in the New Testament; and Ignatius of Antioch acknowledged seven books. Circa AD 108 Polycarp, a personal disciple of the apostle John, acknowledged fifteen New Testament books. Later, Irenaeus (around 130–200), the bishop of Lyon in Gaul (now France), mentioned twenty-two New Testament books, giving special attention to Paul's epistles, which he wrote about more than two hundred times. Finally, Hippolytus of Rome (around 170 to around 236), one of the most prolific writers in early Christianity, recognized twenty-two.

In those days, efforts were occasionally made to compile a canon of scripture. The first known list of New Testament scripture is called the "Muratorian Canon," which was discovered in the eighteenth century and believed to date to the second century. It included all the New Testament books except Hebrews, James, and 3 John. (During that time, those three books, as well as 2 Peter and 2 John, were not yet universally accepted as scripture.)

Acknowledging What Is Already the Truth

As the Christian faith began to expand and churches became more established, the rise in false teachers—as well as some Christians' acceptance of those teachers—moved the faithful leaders in the church to realize that they needed to make a stand against those errors and formally acknowledge which writings were truly the inspired Word of God.

By the beginning of the fourth century, most of the books now in the New Testament had long been treated as scripture. But a few books still required further examination and approval before they could be declared a part of the canon.

Around AD 363, approximately thirty Christian leaders from Asia Minor met at the Council of Laodicea. Among the several items on the agenda at this meeting was the formal adoption of the canon of scripture. This council held that only the Old Testament, including the Apocrypha, and the twenty-seven books in the New Testament to this day could be read in the churches. The Council of Hippo in 393 and the Council of Carthage in 397 followed suit, affirming the same twenty-seven books as the New Testament canon.

These councils didn't arbitrarily choose the twenty-seven books that make up the New Testament, and they didn't just choose the ones they liked best. The process of adopting the canon included putting each "questionable" book through a rigorous five-part test to make certain it deserved a place in the Bible. Here is the essence of each of the five questions asked about each book before it was accepted:

Is the book's author a true apostle or closely connected to one or more of the apostles? For example, Matthew and John, both of whom wrote Gospels included in the canon, were in that group of twelve original apostles whom Jesus appointed. Mark and Luke were not among that group, but they both had close relationships with apostles—Mark with the original Twelve during

Jesus' earthly ministry and later with the apostle Paul; and Luke with Paul, whom Luke accompanied on his last missionary journey (see chapter 1).

Does the body of Christ at large accept the book as inspired? As pointed out earlier, by the time of the councils of Laodicea, Hippo, and Carthage, the church as a whole had already acknowledged most of the scriptures contained in the New Testament as inspired. These writings were already in wide circulation in the churches and were accepted as the Word of God.

Is the book consistent with accepted Christian doctrine? In chapter 2 we discussed how God, through the centuries, has passionately and jealously guarded His written Word against the many possible human errors. When the councils acknowledged the canon of the New Testament, they did so with a keen eye on the message of those books, thus ensuring that no contradictory teachings or doctrines found their way into the canon.

Does the book's content reflect the high moral and spiritual principles that would reflect a work of the Holy Spirit? Many of the books making the rounds in Christian circles at that time reflected a tolerance or acceptance of either the pagan practices or false teachings of the day. The church leaders at these councils knew those things would never pass muster with the teachings of Christ or of the apostles. Only those books that faithfully reflected the character and standards of Christ Himself and of His apostles were considered for inclusion in the canon.

The Canon of Scripture—Who *Really* Decided?

As you've read through this chapter, you've seen some of the events that led to the acceptance of the biblical canon. You've read how what was once a list of countless documents was pared down until it became what we have today: an error-free and contradiction-free Bible that holds perfectly to God's message of salvation for humankind.

How, you may be asking, did such a large number of people—people with the same kinds of flaws and weaknesses we all have today—come to the agreements necessary to produce such a perfect piece of work as the Holy Bible? The answer lies in the guiding hand of God in bringing the process to completion.

All the way through the process of producing the Bible—from the actual writing of the scriptures clear through to the Christian church's recognition of the books God intended to comprise His written Word—you can see the hand of God, working to make sure His message to His people and to a fallen world became exactly what He intended it to be.

No one man or group of men simply *decided* what books would be kept in the canon of scripture and which would be rejected. That happened when God Himself, using the guidance of His Holy Spirit, allowed people to understand which of the books written in the first few centuries of Christianity were truly inspired, or "God-breathed." In other words, the inclusion of the books we have in the Bible today was God's decision and God's work, not man's.

4
Different Languages, Same Message
The Work of Translating the Bible

Down through the centuries, God used gifted and dedicated men to preserve His written Word and keep it true to its original meaning. We can count on the indisputable fact that the message of the Bible has never changed; that it is the same now as it was when first recorded thousands of years ago.

Paraphrasing the prophet Isaiah, the apostle Peter writes, "All flesh is as grass, and all the glory of man as the flower of the grass. The grass withers, and its flower falls away, but the word of the LORD endures forever" (1 Peter 1:24–25). This means that even though people come into and go out of this world, God's commands, promises, and words of encouragement for those who follow Him never change.

What *have* changed, however, are the languages in which God's Word is communicated. Very few people in today's world speak Hebrew or Greek, the languages used to record God's written Word. But God, again using gifted and dedicated men to do His work, has made it possible for people to read and understand the Bible, and to do so in their own languages.

This chapter is dedicated to acknowledging the work of those dedicated souls who committed themselves to making sure the common people could read and understand the Bible. The process started before the birth of Christ, when changes in the language of the Jewish people made it necessary to translate the Hebrew scriptures.

The Septuagint: A Model of Scripture Translation

Centuries before the birth of Jesus Christ, the Hebrew language was all but dead among the common Jewish people living outside of Palestine (now Israel). Though the highly educated Jewish religious leaders of that time understood the language, most Jewish people spoke Greek. For that reason, it was necessary to translate the Hebrew scriptures into Greek.

The translation of the Hebrew scriptures began around 285 BC. This work was called the Septuagint, a name derived from the Latin word for "seventy." One highly doubtful story held that it took the seventy-two translators seventy-two days to finish their work, but in truth, the project took much longer than that.

The translation of the Septuagint was started in Alexandria on the orders of Egyptian King Ptolemy, who wanted the library of Alexandria to include the wisdom literature of all the world's ancient religions. Ptolemy contacted the Jewish chief priest Eleazar and asked him to send Hebrew scholars from Jerusalem to work on the project. Six were chosen from each of the twelve tribes of Israel, which accounts for the accepted number of seventy-two translators. At first, only the Torah (the first five books of the Old Testament) was translated, but eventually the other books were translated and added to the collection. By the time of the birth of Christ, the Septuagint was the translation of the scriptures most Hellenistic (meaning influenced by the Greek culture of the time) Jews used. It was also the text the early churches—which had no New Testament at the time—read from at their gatherings, as well as the text the apostles quoted when they wrote their epistles to various churches.

In time, what we now call the New Testament was written and compiled in Greek. But nearly four centuries later, more changes in language necessitated another key development in the translation of scriptures—both Old Testament and New.

The Bible in the "Common Language"

During Jesus' earthly ministry in Palestine, the common language of the people in that part of the world was Aramaic. But the four Gospels, as well as Paul's letters and other New Testament books, were written in Greek. By late in the fourth century, few people in the Roman Empire could speak or read Greek. By that time, the dominant language in that part of the world was Latin, and that made it necessary for the scriptures to be translated into that language.

Starting early in the third century, parts of the Bible had been translated into Latin, but not the entire Bible, and there were many Latin texts produced, but with little uniformity. Around AD 382, Pope Damasus I, who wanted the church to have a standard version of the Bible, asked a scholar named Jerome (around AD 347–420) to translate the scriptures in their entirety into a uniform Latin text.

Jerome started by revising the Gospels, using then-available Greek manuscripts. Around the same time, he started translating the Old Testament, using the Septuagint as his source. He completed the translation around AD 400, and his version came to be known as the Vulgate, which means "in the common (or vulgar) language of the people."

Jerome's translation was the standard version of the Bible used in the Christian church from the fourth to the fifteenth centuries. There was little additional translating of the Bible during that time, even though the Christian faith spread to non-Latin speaking people—and even though Latin itself faded out in time as the people's spoken and written language. That is mostly because the Catholic Church, which became the supreme authority over the people's religious lives, wouldn't allow anyone to translate the Bible into the languages of the people.

There was a definite need for additional Bible translations, and it was only through the heroic, and very risky, efforts of a few brave individuals that the Bible began being translated into the people's common languages.

Wycliffe Bucks the System

John Wycliffe (sometimes spelled Wyclif or Wycliff) was a gifted theologian and scholar born in Yorkshire, England, in the mid-1320s. He attended Oxford University, where he finished a doctorate in theology in 1372. He later served as a professor at the University of Balliol; and as one of the most distinguished theologians of his time, he served as King Richard II's personal chaplain.

Though Wycliffe was a Catholic priest, he was one of the early dissidents in the Catholic Church. His words and actions later earned him the nickname "Morningstar of the Reformation." When he was in his mid-thirties, Wycliffe began to openly reject and preach against much of the church's erroneous preaching and teaching. For example, he rejected the doctrine that church tradition was equal in authority with the Bible, as well as the infallibility of the pope.

Wycliffe believed that the Bible was the literal, inerrant Word of God. He held that the Bible alone, not the church or any other human institution, was the ultimate authority when it came to the practice of the Christian faith. He also believed that each individual believer had the right and the responsibility to read and interpret the scriptures for himself or herself.

The Roman Catholic Church strictly forbade translation of the Bible into the people's common languages of that time. One enemy of Wycliffe's work summed up the church's position this way: "By this translation, the scriptures have become vulgar, and they are more available to lay [people], and even to women who can read, than they were to learned scholars, who have a high intelligence. So the pearl of the Gospel is scattered and trodden underfoot by swine." But Wycliffe wouldn't be swayed, and he replied to the above by saying, "Englishmen learn Christ's law best in English. Moses heard God's law in his own tongue; so did Christ's apostles."

Wycliffe was well aware that preaching and teaching that all believers should have access to the Bible in their own languages put him at odds with the long-held position of the Catholic Church. But he was willing to risk the wrath of the authorities and move ahead with his plans to translate the Bible into English, an endeavor he began with the help of his close personal friend John Purvey.

With a Little Help from His Friends

Though it was long assumed that the first work of translating the Bible into English was Wycliffe's alone, it is now believed that the "Wycliffite" translations were the result of the efforts of Wycliffe and several other men, including Nicholas of Hereford, John Purvey, and perhaps John Trevisa—all friends and followers of Wycliffe.

The translators worked from the Latin Vulgate. They include in their work what is now the accepted canon of scripture (see chapter 3), as well as several noncanonical texts, which the Reformers (leaders of the Protestant movement such as Martin Luther, John Calvin, and others) later rejected. It is believed that Wycliffe translated the four Gospels himself and that he may have translated the entire New Testament, leaving the translation of the entire Old Testament to his associates after his death.

The work wasn't completed until several years after Wycliffe died of a stroke in 1384. Against the orders of the Catholic Church, Wycliffe's followers—called the Lollards—distributed handwritten copies of the Bible all over England. (This was before the days of the printing press.) Copies of Wycliffe's Bible remained in use for more than a century, until printed Bibles took their place.

Wycliffe was never convicted of heresy for his words or his work (mostly because the church knew that persecuting a man of such popularity in England would likely cause more problems than it could possibly solve), but about thirty years after his death, church authorities had what they thought was the last laugh when they dug up his bones and had them burned and thrown into the Swift River.

Wycliffe's work was just the beginning when it came to Bible translation into English. The Wycliffe Bible had a huge impact on another reformer of the Christian faith, William Tyndale, who took translation of the Bible several more huge steps forward.

William Tyndale: The Father of the English Bible

William Tyndale had everything a young priest needed to take a high and influential position in the Catholic Church. He was fluent in eight languages, and he was proficient in Hebrew and Greek. But Tyndale's true spiritual passion—making it possible for all English-speaking people to read the Bible for themselves—was at great odds with the position the Catholic Church still held.

Tyndale was born in Gloucestershire, England, around 1494, more than a century after the death of his predecessor, John Wycliffe. Like Wycliffe, Tyndale said and did things he knew would get him in trouble with the Catholic Church.

And they most certainly did.

The story is told about how Tyndale responded angrily to an English bishop who stated that the common people didn't need to read the Bible but only needed to rely on the word of the pope. "I defy the pope and all his laws!" Tyndale shouted. "And, if God spares me, I will one day make the boy that drives the plow in England to know more of the scriptures than the pope does!"

Getting the Ball Rolling

Around 1521, Tyndale left the academic world and joined the household of Sir John Walsh in Little Sodbury Manor, north of Bath, where he found himself stunned and saddened at the lack of scriptural knowledge on the part of most of the bishops he met.

During his time at Little Sodbury Manor, Tyndale began receiving reprimands for the things he'd been saying to and about the Catholic clergy. By the summer of 1523, Tyndale knew it was time to move on, so he traveled to London, where he sought permission and funding from Cuthbert Tunstall, the newly appointed bishop of London, to begin his work of translating the New Testament into English.

Tunstall flatly denied Tyndale's request, and Tyndale's efforts to get permission for his project from other authorities were also fruitless. "Not only was there no room in my lord of London's palace to translate the New Testament, but also that there was no place to do it in all of England," he lamented.

Tyndale was discouraged but not defeated. If he couldn't receive the church's blessing for his work, then he was going to move forward without it. He began his work at the home of Humphrey Monmouth, a London merchant who was sympathetic to his cause. When Tyndale's work came to the attention of the English Catholic bishops, he was forced to depart London for Germany, where, with the financial support of Monmouth and other English merchants, he continued his work in a somewhat safer environment.

When in Germany. . .

By the time Tyndale arrived in Germany, Martin Luther had already begun translating the Bible into the German language. During his exile at the Wartburg Castle following the 1521 Diet of Worms, in which he refused to recant his Protestant beliefs, Luther spent his time translating the New Testament into German, using the original Greek text. Luther found that Greek text in the 1516 printed Greek New Testament of Erasmus of Rotterdam, who had translated the New Testament from Greek to Latin himself because he recognized that the Latin Vulgate had become so corrupted. Luther later published a German Pentateuch in 1523. In the 1530s he published the entire Bible in German.

Tyndale planned to use Erasmus's text as his source. He visited with Luther in 1525, and by the end of that year, he had completed his translation of the New Testament. His translation was vastly superior to Wycliffe's, simply because he worked from the original languages of scripture, whereas Wycliffe had worked from the Vulgate, which contained many errors in translation, and which had become more and more degraded over the centuries.

Tyndale and his associates arranged for the Bibles, which he had printed in the German city of Cologne, to be smuggled into England, where they were met with an enthusiastic response from the people—and with rage on the part of the authorities, including King Henry VIII, Cardinal Wolsey, and Sir Thomas More, all of whom claimed that Tyndale's work contained literally thousands of errors in translation. The authorities bought up as many copies of the translation as they could get their hands on—which, ironically, only further financed Tyndale's work—and burned them. They also made plans to stop Tyndale for good.

A Man without a Country

William Tyndale had successfully beaten the centuries-old system and helped make an English translation of the Bible somewhat more available to his countrymen, though Bibles in any language were still hard to come by in those days. But his victories came at great personal cost.

With his New Testaments making their way around England and other parts of the world, Tyndale became a marked man. Though he loved England and missed his friends and family there, he knew it wasn't safe to return to his homeland. For nine years he managed to evade the authorities, while at the same time continuing his work of revising his New Testament and beginning to translate the Old Testament.

Tyndale eventually settled in Antwerp, Belgium, where in 1530 his translation of the Pentateuch (the first five books of the Old Testament) was printed. At that time, he planned to translate the remainder of the Old Testament.

But Tyndale didn't live long enough to realize his dream of an English translation of the complete Bible. In May 1535 Henry Phillips, a fellow Englishman who was actually an agent of the pope, befriended Tyndale. One night Phillips lured Tyndale out to the streets of Antwerp, where he was arrested and then taken to a prison cell in the castle of Vilvorde, near Brussels. In August 1536 Tyndale was condemned as a heretic, and on October 6 of that year, he was given a chance to recant. When he refused, he was hanged and his body burned at the stake.

Picking Up Where Tyndale Left Off

Miles Coverdale, the English Bishop of Exeter, and John Rogers, a protestant English minister, were William Tyndale's faithful allies during the final six years of his life, and they remained faithful to working toward accomplishing his goal of making an English Bible available for the people to read.

After Tyndale's death, Coverdale completed the translation of the Old Testament, and in 1535 he printed the first complete Bible in the English language, the Coverdale Bible. Two years later Rogers printed the second complete English Bible, this one translated directly from Hebrew and Greek and called Matthew's Bible, after "Thomas Matthew," which is thought to be a pseudonym for John Rogers.

In 1539 Thomas Cranmer, Archbishop of Canterbury, employed Coverdale—at the direction of King Henry VIII—to publish what is now known as the Great Bible, due to its huge size (around fourteen inches thick). The Great Bible, which Coverdale himself published, was the first English Bible authorized for public use. In 1541 Henry ordered that a copy of the Great Bible be placed in every parish. Though the English church still held that the "common" people weren't allowed to possess their own copies of the Bible or to read them on their own (under penalty of imprisonment), Coverdale's work brought English Christians a step closer to being allowed to own and read the Bible for themselves.

A Big Step Backward

Though Henry VIII, who broke with the Catholic Church and embraced Protestantism, allowed men such as Coverdale and Rogers to translate the Bible into English, and even sanctioned and financed their work, this newfound freedom didn't last. After Henry's death, King Edward VI took the throne. After Edward's death, Mary Tudor, a devout Catholic, assumed rule in England. "Bloody" Mary wanted to return England to Roman Catholic rule, and she began a wave of persecution against Protestant reformers and Bible translators, including John Rogers and Thomas Cranmer, who were both burned at the stake as heretics in 1555.

During that time, the Protestant Church at Geneva, Switzerland, became a safe haven for exiled English Protestants, including

Miles Coverdale. These Protestant exiles wanted to produce a Bible in the English language for their families to read while they were in exile. In 1560, while working under the protection of John Calvin, the leader of the Geneva church, they published the Geneva Bible, a complete translation into English compiled by William Whittingham, Anthony Bilbey, Thomas Sampson, Christopher Goodman, and William Cole.

Getting the entire Bible printed in the language of the people required immense sacrifice on the part of several individuals. But the time would come when the Catholic Church relaxed its iron-fisted control over the scriptures—and over who could possess and read them. When that finally happened, it opened the door for the bestselling, most-beloved version of the Bible ever printed: the King James Version.

5
The Rise of the All-Time Bestseller
The King James Version and
Other Modern Translations

After the death of Mary Tudor in 1558, her half sister, Elizabeth I, ascended to the throne of England. In 1559 the English Parliament revoked the Catholicism of the previous monarchy. In 1563 what is called the "Elizabethan Settlement" reestablished the Church of England.

With Queen Mary out of the way, the once-exiled English reformers returned to their homeland, where they could now live in relative safety. The Church of England—also known as the Anglican Church—at that time reluctantly tolerated the printing and distribution of the Geneva Bible, even though the marginal notes in the work were vehemently against the institutional church of the day.

Church of England leaders wanted a new version of the Bible, one without what they considered inflammatory marginal notes. Under Elizabeth I, the Great Bible was again placed in the churches. In 1568 a revision of the Great Bible—called the Bishop's Bible, which church leaders considered a more literal translation than the Great Bible—was printed and distributed. Nineteen editions of the Bishop's Bible, which has been referred to as "the rough draft of the King James Version," made it to print between 1568 and 1606, but none of them were popular with the people.

In 1582 the Catholic Church in England, more than anything seeing the futility of clinging to the centuries-long Latin-only law of Bible translation, particularly in a Protestant nation, changed its tune and allowed the printing of Bibles in English, and even printed an official Roman Catholic English Bible. Using the badly distorted Vulgate as its source, the church published an English Bible that had been translated in a Catholic college in the city of Rheims: the Rheims New Testament. Later, in 1609, the Catholic Church published the Douay Old Testament, which was translated at a college in the city of Douay. The two were later combined, producing a Bible called the Douay-Rheims Version.

Though the English Protestants had it far better under Elizabeth than they had under Mary Tudor, there was an undercurrent of conflict, namely between more traditional Anglicans and more radical Protestants who came to be known as "Puritans."

The conflicts between the Church of England and the Puritans continued through the reign of Elizabeth's successor, King James I, and they played an important part in another pivotal moment in the history of Bible translation. It was a part King James himself is most remembered for to this day.

A "Crowning" Achievement

King James I (born on June 19, 1566, as James Charles Stuart) was the son of Mary Queen of Scots and Lord Darnley, who was murdered before James's first birthday. Crowned at one year of age, James served as king of Scotland (as James VI) for thirty-six years before ascending to the throne of England in 1603, after the death of Elizabeth I.

James I accomplished his lifelong dream of uniting England, Scotland, and Ireland into what he called "Great Britain." But he began his reign during a time of some long-festering religious conflicts in his kingdom, which he attempted to resolve when he called the Hampton Court Conference in mid-January 1604.

At the conference, English Christian leaders were allowed to air their differences and present what they believed were problems within English Christianity. One of those leaders was John Reynolds, the president of Corpus Christi College in Oxford and a Puritan, who told the court that a new and improved translation of the Bible into English was needed—one free of marginal notes (like those in the Geneva Bible) and one that held absolutely true to the original languages of scripture.

Although the Bible hadn't been placed on the court's official agenda, James I listened to and agreed with Reynolds, and he wasted little time in getting started on what would become the bestselling book of all time.

Men at Work—*Hard* Work!

By July 1604 James I had appointed fifty-four of the world's most-renowned Bible scholars and linguists of the day to translate the Bible. Each had a solid grasp on the Hebrew, Greek, and Aramaic languages, and each had written, translated, and edited works in Greek. And each, most importantly, was a Christian man with a passion for the Word of God.

Though fifty-four men were appointed to the task, just forty-seven of them are known to have actually taken part in the work. The translators were divided into six groups—two working at Oxford, two at Cambridge, and two at Westminster—with each group taking responsibility for one section of scripture. They translated from the best Greek and Hebrew manuscripts available at the time, and they also made use of commentaries and earlier English translations. As they worked, they held to fifteen rules for translation, all of which were laid out to ensure that the finished product was an absolutely literal translation from the Hebrew and Greek of the original scriptures into English.

It was painstaking work, completed over a period of several years. Each individual in a group translated the same portion of scripture, and then went over it again until he was satisfied that it was faithful to the original meaning and wording. He then submitted his portion to the rest of his group, which discussed it and decided which translation was the best. When a particular book of the Bible was completed, it was then submitted to the other groups to be examined again. Questions one group had about a particular point were then sent back to the group responsible for the translation. Any disagreements on the text were settled at a meeting of the leaders of each group.

The work, which came to be known as the King James Version, or the Authorized Version, was completed and issued in 1611, with a complete title page reading:

> The HOLY BIBLE, Conteyning the Old Testament, and the New: Newly Translated out of the Original tongues: & with the former Translations diligently compared and revised, by his Majesties Special Commandment. Appointed to be read in Churches. Imprinted at London by Robert Barker, Printer to the Kings most Excellent Majestie. Anno Dom. 1611.

In time, the Authorized Version (called that even though there is no record of it being authorized by anyone in power) of the Bible would take its place as the most loved and influential piece of literature of all time. To this day, it remains the world's best-selling book, and it is still praised for its accuracy in holding to the original Bible manuscripts and for its literary qualities.

The Authorized Version Takes Its Place

It wasn't long before the King James Version (KJV) replaced the Great Bible as the version used in church parishes throughout

England. In Scotland, churches still used the Geneva Bible until 1633, when a Scottish edition of the Authorized Version was printed, and it soon took the Geneva Bible's place in the churches.

The general public was slower to accept the KJV, favoring the Geneva Bible for a few decades after the first printing of the KJV. Large numbers of the Geneva Bible found their way into England from Amsterdam, where printing of the "outdated" Bibles continued until around 1644. The printing of the Geneva editions slowed and then ceased in England after 1616, and in 1633 Archbishop Laud of Canterbury prohibited both their printing and their importation. By the end of the seventeenth century, the KJV had become the only current version of the Bible circulating among English-speaking people.

Over time, the King James Version went through some revisions of its own, including those done in the seventeenth and eighteenth centuries to correct printing errors, which were oftentimes the result of carelessness in the publishing process. Two editions completed in Cambridge—in 1629 and 1638—attempted to restore the original text and also introduced more than two hundred revisions of the original translators' work.

By the end of the eighteenth century, the Authorized Version was, for all practical purposes, the only Bible used in English-speaking Protestant churches. In 1752 the Catholic Church in England printed a revision of the Douay-Rheims Version that was very close in content to the Authorized Version. The KJV also took the Vulgate's place as the Bible that English-speaking scholars and church leaders used for their work.

Along with Johannes Gutenberg's development of the printing press, the translation of the King James Version remains one of the pivotal developments in the history of Bible translation and publication. But work on "updating" the Bible didn't stop with the KJV. Though the Authorized Version maintained its place as the bestselling Bible of all time, over the four centuries since its completion, the work of making the Bible readable to more people has continued, resulting in a wide variety of translations of God's Word into our spoken language.

Picking Up Where the KJV Left Off

All you have to do to understand that the English language has changed over the centuries is crack open a copy of the King James Version and start reading. Though the content and meaning of the Bible text are the same as they were when they were written, changes in how we speak and read necessitated changes in how God's Word is presented.

Beginning in 1881, a group of English and American scholars created a new translation called the Revised Version (or English Revised Version), which was intended as a revision of the King James Version, adapting the Bible text to updated English usage.

At the time of the publication of the entire Revised Version in 1885, the King James Version was still the best English Bible translation—both in terms of accuracy and style. The RV translation included elements not seen in the KJV, including arrangement of the text into paragraphs, printing of Old Testament poetry (such as the Psalms) in indented poetic lines, and the addition of marginal notes to point out to the reader variations in wording in ancient manuscripts. For these reasons, the RV is considered the forerunner of all modern Bible translations.

In 1900 Thomas Nelson & Sons, an American publishing company, released the American Standard Version (ASV) Old Testament, and the following year the publishing company published the complete ASV Bible. The work on the ASV began in 1872, with thirty American and British scholars, chosen by the Swiss theologian Philip Schaff, doing their work using much of the work already done on the Revised Version. One of the most notable differences between the Revised Version and the ASV is that the latter uses a more Americanized style of the English language.

The ASV became the basis of four twentieth-century revisions of the Bible: the Revised Standard Version (released in 1952), the Amplified Bible (1965), the New American Standard Bible (1971), and the Recovery Version (1999). It was also the basis for a popular paraphrase called The Living Bible (1971).

The Bible in the Twentieth and Twenty-first Centuries

The translation of the Bible into more updated English continued throughout the twentieth century and continues to this day, with several versions introduced since the early 1950s.

Below are some of the more popular versions published since the beginning of the twentieth century:

The Revised Standard Version (RSV)—Printed in its entirety in 1952 (the New Testament was published in 1946), the RSV was a comprehensive revision of the KJV, the RV, and the ASV. The RSV, which aimed to be a more readable but still accurate English translation of the original Bible texts, posed the first serious challenge to the popularity of the KJV.

The Amplified Bible (1965)—The first Bible project of the Lockman Foundation, this translation helps the reader understand what scripture really says and really means by taking into account both word meaning and context. This is accomplished by the use of synonyms and definitions in order to "amplify" the meaning of Bible texts.

New American Standard Bible (NASB)—Like so many Bible translations before and since, the purpose of the NASB, which was published in its entirety in 1971, was to update the grammar and terminology of scripture while at the same time staying true to the original texts. Scholars worked for ten years translating from the best available Bible texts.

The Living Bible (TLB)—American author Kenneth N. Taylor was once quoted as saying that he paraphrased the American Standard Version of the Bible in order to make the Bible readable and understandable to the average reader, including children, which he said were his inspiration for his work. The result was The Living Bible, which was released in 1971. Billy Graham used portions of The Living Bible in his evangelistic crusades. This version was the bestselling Bible in the United States in the early 1970s.

Today's English Version (TEV), or Good News Bible (GNB)—The American Bible Society first published the New Testament of this version, titled *Good News for Modern Man*, in 1966, with American and British editions of the complete Bible following in 1976. Working to provide a faithful translation of the original texts into clear, concise, modern English, a committee of Bible scholars translated the original texts they had available into this version.

New International Version (NIV)—This version was conceived in 1965, when years of study by committees from the Christian Reformed Church and the National Association of Evangelicals, an international, trans-denominational group of scholars, concluded that a new translation into contemporary English was needed. The NIV was a result of the work of more than one hundred scholars working from the best available Hebrew, Aramaic, and Greek texts. The NIV New Testament was released in 1973, with the complete NIV Bible following in 1978.

New King James Version (NKJV)—In 1975 Thomas Nelson Publishers commissioned the work for the NKJV, which was intended to be a Bible with the exact content of the KJV, only with updated language (for example, old English pronouns such as "thou," "thee," "ye," and "thine" were changed to reflect modern English). One hundred thirty respected Bible scholars, church leaders, and others worked seven years to complete this project, which was published in its entirety in 1982, three years after the release of the NKJV New Testament.

New Living Translation (NLT)—The NLT is the result of what started out as an effort to revise The Living Bible, but it evolved into an altogether new translation of the Bible. Beginning in 1989, a team of eighty-seven translators began working on the NLT, and the work was completed and published in 1996.

The Message (MSG)—The pastor, scholar, and writer Eugene H. Peterson created *The Message: The Bible in Contemporary Language* to help people in his Bible study classes better connect with the vital, life-changing message of the Bible. *The Message* is a paraphrase of the original languages of the Bible, not a literal word-for-word translation. Navpress Publishers began publishing segments of *The Message* Bible in 1993, and the complete Bible became available in 2002.

Holman Christian Standard Bible (HCSB)—In 2004 Holman Bible Publishers released the HCSB, which is a version of the Bible using both dynamic and formal equivalence, meaning some of the text is translated word for word, while some of it is translated with the goal of conveying the actual thought behind the words.

Which is the Best of the Best?

With all these Bible translations and paraphrases so readily available, the question that so often arises is this: Which one is best?

Which translation or version most faithfully represents the true original message of scripture is a source of constant debate among spiritual leaders as well as Bible scholars. Some hold that most of the versions listed in the previous section, as well as the King James Version itself, are all solid works that faithfully communicate the intended message of the original scriptures. Others hold a narrower view, stating that the KJV and a few others are the only truly accurate renderings of the original. Still others hold the even narrower view that the KJV is the only translation that is absolutely true to the original manuscripts.

The bottom line is that there are several excellent versions of the Bible available, and which one you choose for your personal reading and studies should depend on two important factors. First, which version do you find easier to follow and understand? You will find your Bible reading much more fruitful when you can follow the language used well enough to fully grasp what it is saying to you. Second, when you go shopping for a Bible, begin by praying and asking God to guide you to the version that is best for you. As with anything else in your life of faith, God knows better than anyone what you really need, and that includes which version of the Bible you should be reading.

If you enjoyed

YOUR
BIBLE

be sure to look for these other great Bible
resources from Barbour Publishing!

The Complete Guide to the Bible
7" x 9½", Paperback, 512 pages
ISBN 978-1-59789-374-9

500 Questions & Answers from the Bible
6" x 9", paperback, 256 pages
ISBN 978-1-59789-473-9

Bible Atlas & Companion
8" x 10", paperback, 176 pages
ISBN 978-1-59789-779-2

Available wherever Christian books are sold.